KNOW YOUR COUNTRY

AND

BEYOND

KNOW YOUR COUNTRY

AND

BEYOND

AHMADU KURFI

Safari Books Ltd., Ibadan

Published by
Safari Books Ltd
Cambridge House
20 Joop Berkhout Crescent
Onireke, Ibadan
Email: safarinigeria@gmail.com

© Ahmadu Kurfi OFR
Publisher: Chief Joop Berkhout OON
Deputy Publisher: George Berkhout

Know Your Country and Beyond
Published 2011

All rights reserved. This book is copyright and so no part of it may be reproduced, stored in a retrieval system, or transmitted, in any form or by any means, electronic, mechanical, electrostatic, magnetic tape, photocopying, recording or otherwise, without the prior written permission of the author.

ISBN: 978-978-8431-07-7

DEDICATION

To the teachers who taught me at the following Alma Maters; Central Elementary School (CES) Katsina (1941 – 1944) - Malam Magaji Daura, Malam Iro Gawo (Senior Visiting Teacher), Malam Dan Malam Karofi (Headmaster), Malam Amadu Kumasi (Visiting Teacher).

Katsina Middle School (1944 – 1947) - Malam Iro Mashi (Headmaster), Malam Iro Yamel, Malam Labo Kankia, Malam Usman Iya Iyai, Malam Hassan Rafindadi, Malam Gado, Malam Musa Yaradua, Malam Abdu Randawa, Malam Abdulrahman Rafindadi, Malam Abdulrahman Masanawa.

Kaduna College, Zaria Secondary School (Now Barewa College, 1947– 1950) - A.W.A Spicer (Awas) Principal, Mr. White house, Malam Yahaya Gusau, Malam Isa Koto, Malam Abdulrahman Mora (MM), Mr. J.M Beckley, Mr. Onimole (Oga), Mr. S.V Baker, Malam Aliyu Mai Bornu, Malam Dodo Mustapha, Malam Halliru Binji, Mr. Russel, Mr. J.W. Court, Mr. Ridley, Mr. Edward Arthur, Mr Austin, Mr. Dawson.

Higher Elementary (Teachers) Training Centre, Katsina (1951 – 1952) - J.J. Williams (Principal), Mr. Picton Hughes, Mr. Alexander Petigrew, Malam Maiwada Zaria. Hull University, England (1955 – 1958) - Bryan Jones -Vice Chancellor, Professor Ian Bowen, Professor King, Mr. Kemp.

And several other teachers whose names do not appear amongst those listed, but who, like them, imparted in me knowledge, discipline, deportment and other desireable attributes which make me what I am and became later in life. I thank them all and may their gentle souls rest in perfect peace, Amen.

FOREWORD

It is quite an uncommon request to receive a bulky manuscript preparatory to its publication into a book bestowing one with the privilege of writing a foreword from the Palace of a Royal Father who should have ordinarily been preoccupied with the challenges of administering his domain on the one hand and basking in the perks and perquisites of royalties on the other. This common place expectations are not trappings that could dominate and stunt a virile mind which Allah (SWT) has in His mercy blessed the Maradin Katsina, Alhaji Ahmadu Kurfi with.

The General Study Programme (GSP) papers presented to selected secondary school students by Maradin Katsina, Alhaji Ahmadu Kurfi that are put together to constitute this book are not only rich and diversified in content but lucid in their flow; a clear testimony of a robust mind at work. The content of this book traversing history, sociology, geography, economy and issues of politics and constitutionalism in classical and contemporary contexts should be a reference material not only for secondary school students but for anybody interested in concretely knowing the general systematic evolution of our environment. Indeed, while the subjects treated are in some instances specific, the overall content meets the theme and essence of the book as a general study compendium. Not surprisingly, the level of articulation of the book could, in my judgement, stand any intellectual rating.

Apart from the substances and ideas embedded in the materials of this book, Maradin Katsina has by this endeavour thrown a challenge to his generation to translate accumulated experience into intellectual enterprise through marrying their empirical-cum-pragmatic background with the subtlety of acquired training in conceptual and theoretical analysis. In another vein, this kind of effort will certainly serve as a beacon and reference point to up coming generation to imbibe the virtues of learning, working, serving and imparting.

I sincerely thank Maradin Katsina, Alhaji Ahmadu Kurfi for giving me the honour to write this foreword, thereby earning a place in this book that will remain in the societal collection of literature from an author with the rare traces of administrative experience, intellectual grooming ensconced in the secure recesses of royalty.

Dr. Ibrahim Shehu Shema, *Fnim*
(Sarakin Yakin Hausa)
Governor, Katsina State
2010

PREFACE

The book titled - Know Your Country and beyond, is a collection of notes which formed the basis of lectures which I delivered as part of a General Study Programme (GSP).

The lectures were delivered to Senior Classes 1 - 3 and Junior Class 3. The theme of the lectures was Know Your Country and Beyond. The lectures were delivered at the following Secondary Schools located in Kurfi Local Government Area, Katsina State of Nigeria. :-

    Government Rural Boarding/Day Secondary School, Kurfi
    Day Secondary School, Birchi
    Day Secondary School, Rawayau
    Day Secondary School, Tsauri
    Community Girls Arabic Secondary School, Kurfi
    Fatima Memorial Islamic College, Kurfi.

The theme of the lectures was Know Your.................... delivered in stages as follows:-

Lecture   1 - Know Your Local Government, Kurfi
               2 - Know Your State, Katsina
               3 - Know Your Country, Nigeria
               4 - Know Your Continent, Africa
               5 - Know Your World
               6 - Know The Universe

The delivery of lectures at monthly or longer intervals began on 24th February 2009 and ended on 22nd January 2010.

The contents of each lecture included, but not limited to the following topics:-

Creation / Establishment, Size of ; Land Area; Physical features such as Rivers, Mountains, Lakes, Seas, Oceans etc; Agriculture and Natural Resources; Administration, History, Political Economy, other prominent topics etc. Teachers, pupils, students, of the schools visited benefited from the lectures which were intended to widen their horizon about their immediate environment, and beyond.

What motivated me to conceive the General Study Programme was the utter dearth of knowledge of both teachers and students of their immediate environment, their State, Nigeria, Africa and the World at large. An average educated person ought to be cognisant of geography, history, politics, economy etc., of his environment and beyond. It is hoped that with the publication of this book, local, state and federal governments will initiate similar General Study Programmes with a view to broadening knowledge of lecturers, teachers and students to become really educated and contribute more meaningfully to the development of their country.

ALHAJI (Dr) AHMADU KURFI OFR,
MARADIN KATSINA, HAKIMIN KURFI.

TABLE OF CONTENTS

Dedication   *v*
Foreword   *vii*
Preface   *viii*
Acknowledgements   *xiii*

Chapter One

Know your Local Government -Kurfi.............................. 1
Population 3
Agricultural Produce 4
Water Supply................................ 5
Educational Development 6
Health Care 7

Chapter Two

Know Your State -Katsina 11
Brief History of Katsina State 11
Population 15
Education 18
Health Care Development 19
Mineral Resources 23
Military and Civilian Administrations 24
Katsina the Great Province 28
Ministry of Education Katsina State 32

Chapter Three

Know your Country -Nigeria 51
Brief History 51
The Modern Development of Politics 56
Independence 61
The Economy 66

Education	69
Elections	70
Mining	71
Manufacturing	72
Energy	73
Transportation	74
Communication	75
Currency and Banking	76
Administration	76

Chapter Four

Know Your Continent - Africa	113
Climatic Zones	120
People of Africa	123
Education	127
Mining	129
Energy	130
West Africa to the 1870s	131
Jihads and New States in 19th Century West Africa	132
Abolition of the Slave Trade	134
Conquest of a Continent	137
Colonial Rule	140
Africa and the World Wars	146
The Winning of Independence	147
Africa and the World Economy	152
Organisation of African Unity (OAU)	155

Chapter Five

Know the World	163
Ancient Rome	163
Origin of the Crusades	167
British Empire	176
Colonialism and Colonies	179
World War I	180
World War II	184
Formation of the Axis of Coalition	187

Chapter Six

Know the Universe 217
The Sun 220
Space Flight 224

List Of Tables And Figures

Table 2.1: Educational Development in Katsina State 35
Table 2.2: List of Existing Principal/Major Dams in
    Katsina State 40
Table 2.3: Major Industries in Katsina State 43
Table 2.4: Names and Dates of Dynasties in Katsina 44
Table 2.5: List of Kings and Queens of Daura 46
Table 2.6: Daura Fulani King List 49
Table 2.7: Result of Katsina Population Census of 2006 50
Table 3.1: Local Government Areas in Nigeria 78
Table 3.2: Result of 2006 Population Census 86
Table 3.3: Population by Local Government Area and Sex 87
Table 3.4: States and their Dates of Creation in Nigeria 111
Table 4.1: Population of Countries in Africa 160
Table 5.1: Countries and their Sizes 201
Table 5.2: Countries and their Population 206
Table 5.3: Deserts and their Sizes 209
Table 5.4: Rivers and their Lengths 210
Table 5.5: World Production of Food and Cash Crops 213
Table 5.6: World Natural Resources 215
Table 6.1: Lunar Data 225
Table 6.2: Physical and Astronomical Data of Earth's
    Solar System 226

Figure 1.1: Map of Kurfi 9
Figure 2.1: Map of Katsina State 27
Figure 3.1: Map of Nigeria showing the 36 states and Abuja 68
Figure 4.1: Map of Africa 141
Figure 5.1: Map of the World 200

ACKNOWLEDGEMENTS

The basic facts used for this book were culled from the notes I used for the lectures delivered by me at various secondary schools located in Kurfi Local Government Area, Katsina State of Nigeria.

In the preparation of these notes, extensive use was made of published materials produced by ministries, departments, agencies (MDAs) of Local, State and Federal Governments of Nigeria, which they made available to me. The sources have been indicated in the book. I am grateful to the management and staff of these MDAS.

The author and publishers also wish to thank individuals, corporate entities, non-governmental organisations (NGOs) at local, regional and international levels for kind permission to print from their respective publications, extract included in this book. Sources from these publications and the internet are acknowledged in the book.

I am grateful to the various authors, producers of the publications from which extracts are included in this book with their kind permission, particularly Microsoft @ Encarta, 2009, @1993 Microsoft corporation, which provided useful information and data on their website for inclusion in this book.

Ahmadu Kurfi
Maradin Katsina

CHAPTER ONE

Know Your Local Government-Kurfi

Kurfi Local Government was created by the Babangida Military Administration on 23rd September, 1991. It was carved out from Dutsinma Local Government Area, and Kurfi District which is conterminous with the Local Government Area was also curved out from Dutsinma District.

At its inception, Kurfi District comprised the following Village Areas;-

> Kurfi Village Area headed by Magajin Garin Kurfi;
> Tsauri Village Area headed by Magaji Tsauri;
> Wurma Village Area headed by Magaji Wurma;
> Rawayau Village Area headed by Magaji Rawayau;
> Birchi Village Area headed by Magaji Birchi;
> Kufan Agga Village Area headed by Magaji Kufan Agga.

Alhaji Ahmadu Kurfi was appointed Maradin Katsina, Hakimin Kurfi, District Head by Emir of Katsina, Alhaji (Dr) Muhammadu Kabir Usman, on 4th June, 1992. Following reorganization of Administrative Units in Katsina Emirate in 1999, the number of Village Areas was increased from six to twelve with the addition of the following Village Heads ;-

1. Magaji Sharu
2. Magaji Kaware
3. Magaji Tamu
4. Magaji Tamawa
5. Magaji Sabon Gari
6. Magaji Gwanzo.

Structure Of Local Government

Kurfi LG comprises the following ten electoral Wards -

Kurfi A, Kurfi B
Tsauri A, Tsauri B
Wurma A, Wurma B
Rawayau A, Rawayau B
Birchi Ward
Barkiya Ward.

Each Ward elects a councillor to represent it at the Local Government Council which is headed by Honourable Chairman of the Council who is elected by the whole Local Government Area.

Also, there are Supervisory Councillors who are appointed by the Chairman after due consultations with relevant stakeholders. These supervisory Councillors supervise departments of the Local Government which include the following;-

Agriculture
Works
Health
Education and Social Welfare
Administration and

Treasury.

Each department is headed by Head of Department (HOD) under whom there are Unit Heads.

The local government bureaucracy is headed by Director of Administration and Finance (DAF) who is Head of Service and coordinates the activities of the Departmental Heads.

Chairman and Councillors are elected for a three year term.

Local Education Authority (L.E.A)

This semi-autonomous department is responsible for the recruitment, promotion, compensation and discipline of teachers deployed to the 72 primary schools in the LGA. The department is responsible to the State Universal Basic Education Board (SUBEB) which supervises the activities of the LEA headed by the Education Secretary who is appointed for a five year term by the Council Chairman, subject to approval by the State Government.

Population - 117,581 (male 60,625, female 56,959) according to Population Census 2006. Land Area 576.7 Sq Km.

Kurfi Local Government Area has common borders with;- Dutsinma LGA to the South, Batagarawa to the North, Charanchi to the East, Batsari to the West and Safana to the Southwest. The following rivers traverse Kurfi LGA;- Gulbin Gada or Gulbin Kurfi, Rairaye, Chidawaki as well as minor rivers, brooks and streams.

The People;- Almost entirely Hausa and Fulani who are Muslims. They are farmers and cattle herders.

Agricultural Produce;- sorghum/guinea corn (Dawa) millet (Gero), maize (Masara), groundnuts (Gyada), beans (Wake), Beni seed (Ridi). Sweet Potatoes (Dankali), cassava (Rogo), pumpkin (Kabewa, Duma), Kubewa, Kuka etc. A host of other crops are grown in small quantities in various parts of the LGA. The animals being reared include cows, sheep and goats as well birds such as chickens, guinea fowls, ducks, and pigeons. Sale of surplus farm produce as well as animals and birds provide cash to meet daily need of families.

Roads;- Major federal and state roads pass through Kurfi town - They are;-

Katsina - Kurfi - Dutsinma - Kankara - Kaduna road;
Kurfi - Charanchi - Kano road;
Kurfi - Katsina road;
Kurfi - Batsari - Jibia road.

There are also numerous laterite roads constructed by the local government that criss -cross the Local Government Area. Among these are;-

Kurfi - Kaware - Tsauri road
Kurfi - Birchi - Rawayau road
Kurfi - Birchi - Wurma road
Kurfi - Yar Randa - Takabawa road
Kurfi - Tamawa road
Kurfi - Kaguwa - Tamu road
Kaware — Gwanzo road

Electricity;- Kurfi town and the following villages have been connected to the electricity National grid - Rawayau, Birchi, Wurma, Barkiya Tamawa, Kaware, Tsauri, Tamu, Gwanzo, Sabon Gari.

Water Supply;- Kurfi town is connected with potable public water supply under the Semi - Urban Water Supply scheme of the Katsina State Government but funded by Kurfi Local Government Council. The water is pumped from Dan Nakwari Village reservoir. The Local Government has also constructed concrete wells and boreholes in various parts of the LGA. The boreholes are operated by solar power or hand pumps.

Brief History;- Although each of the original six village areas has its peculiar history, that of Kurfi, Sharu, Tamawa, Kufan Agga has been recorded in Alhaji Ahmadu's autobiography and is briefly as follows.

Malam Yusufu was given a flag at Birnin Gada. He reigned for nine years fighting the Katsina Habe. He was killed at GARABI. That's why Kurfi people are called GARABAWA. After he was killed, his eldest son Alu was appointed Maradi. He ruled for four years. He was killed at Birnin Maradi at MARAKA. Then Maradi Jabbo was appointed in the Birnin Maradi Area. He was driven away (from there), and he settled at RIRRIMI, west of Zakka. During the rebellion of Dan Mari (1842 - 1844 AD), he moved to Kafin Soli. From there, he was moved to Kurfi which was built for him on the instruction of Sarkin Musulmi. He reigned for forty-two years. He was succeeded by Maradi Mamman Mai geme who reigned for nineteen years. The latter was followed by Mani Dan Jatau (Mamman's younger brother) who ruled for five months. Mani Maidan Jatau was followed by Albarka, son of Jabbo who reigned for eight months. He too was succeeded by Maradi Sani son of Jabbo who ruled for thirty-eight years, followed by me (Alu son for Sani and as at today 1952) he reigned for thirty-five years.

Maradi Alu II, my father, died on 7th October 1964, having ruled for forty-six years from 1918. Hence, the Maradi Dynasty of Kurfi ruled for total of one hundred and sixty-two years by the time Maradi Alu II died. Since duration of the reigns were recorded in Islamic lunar years, One hundred and sixty-two Lunar years converts to approximately one hundred and fifty-five years of Gregorian calendar. As at 2009, the dynasty has ruled for two hundred years.

According to Mdaradi Alu (Aliyu), Malam Yusufu Nagarabi, Umarun Dumyawa, Ummarun Dallaje, Na Alhaji Duk Almajiran Shehu Danfodio Ne, that is to say, the four gentlemen were all Shehu Danfodio's pupils or disciples. All these leaders participated in the jihad (holy war) and each was given a flag by Shehu, the Amirul Muminin (commander of the faithful) to command expeditions against the Habe rulers of Katsina.

Educational Development

The first elementary (primary) school was built in Kurfi town (on the site of present day Model Primary School) in 1949 to be followed by the construction of Tsauri Elementary School in 1960. Today there are 72 Primary Schools in Kurfi Local Government with a total enrolment of 18,257 comprising 9953 males and 8304 females, being taught by 471 teachers. There are also;-

143 Islamiyya schools with a total enrolment of 4164 Pupils 126 Koranic schools with a total enrolment of 2625 Pupils. There are 251 teachers in the Islamic schools and 124 teachers in Koranic schools.

The first secondary school was established at Kurfi town in 1982 to be followed by another at Birchi Village in 1984.

Today there are ten secondary schools located as follows;-

4 Schools at Kurfi - Government Rural Boarding and Day Secondary Schools, Senior and Junior Sections (two schools).

Community Arabic Girls Secondary School and Fatima Memorial Islamic Collage, two Day secondary schools at Birchi — Junior and Senior sections; one Day secondary school at Rawayau, one Day secondary school at Tsauri, one Day secondary school at Wurma, one Day secondary school at Tamawa.

There are also:

a) 143 Islamiyya schools with a total enrolment of 4164 pupils being taught by 251 teachers;

b) 126 Koranic schools with an enrolment of 2625 pupils being taught by 124 teachers.

Health Care

The first dispensary was built at Kurfi town in 1949. Today, there are;

One general hospital at Kurfi;
One comprehensive health centre each at Rawayau, Tsauri, Wurma, Barkiya. Additionally, there are 34 health facilities at various villages in the local government area.

State Government Agencies:

General Hospital, Sharia Court, Secondary Schools etc.

Federal Government Agencies:
  Nigeria Police;
  State Security Services;
  Immigration Services;
  National Security and Civil Defence Corps.

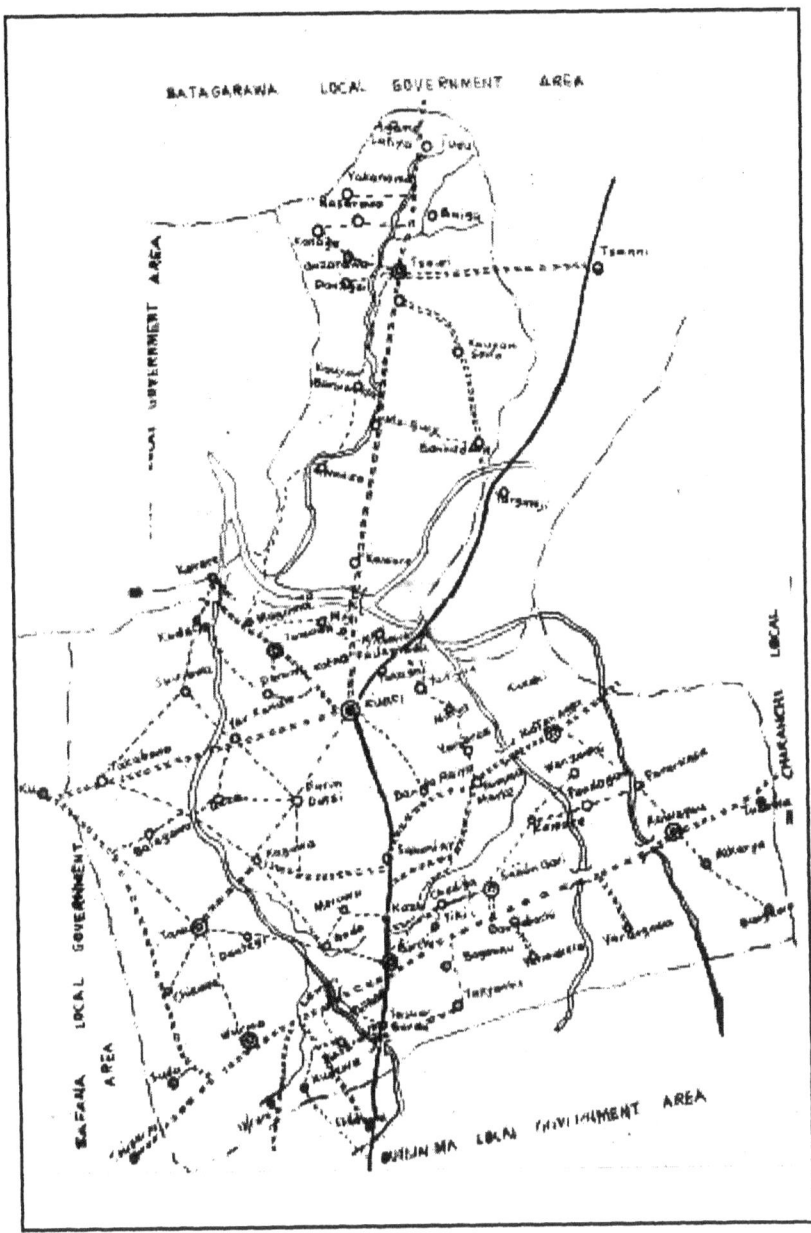

Figure 1.1: Map of Kurfi Local Government Area and Its Environ

CHAPTER TWO

Know Your State - Katsina

Katsina State was created by the Babangida Military Administration on Wednesday, 27th September, 1987. It was carved out from Kaduna State. With the creation of Katsina and Akwa Ibom States, the Nigerian Federation comprised twenty-one federating units and this number was increased to;-

30 states in 1991 (Babangida Administration)
36 States in 1996 (Abacha Administration).

Brief History Of Katsina State

Katsina State is a geographical and political expression of an area that comprises two ancient Kingdoms of Katsina and Daura. These Kingdoms are among the oldest seven Hausa City States. Others are Kano, Gobir, Zazzau, Rano and Biram (Garun Gabas) which formed the original Hausaland, the habitats of the Negroid stock of Berber-Afro-Asiatic group of people called Hausawa. The area is located in the Sahel Savannah region of Northern Nigeria between Kano and Sokoto. Its principal neighbours are Zamfara and Sokoto States to the West, Jigawa and Kano to the East, while Maradi and Damagaram in Niger Republic lie to the North and Northeast. Zariya in Kaduna State lies to the South. Historical accounts indicate that the kingdoms of Katsina and Daura had, at a certain period, comprised a wide area and great stretches of land from north to south, with spheres of influence transcending the current state's borders. The territories of Korgom, Kance, Tasawa, Maradi, Kanenbakashe, Jiratawa, Sumanana, Madarunfa in Niger Republic had formerly been the northern parts of these kingdoms. The spheres of influence of Katsina in particular had once comprised the areas of Birnin Gwari, Karaushi, Kirrisen, Madauchi, Kuyambana and the marshlands of Sangiyakun in present Kaduna, Kebbi and Niger States. Its territories in the west comprised 'Yandoto, Tsafe, Kwatarkwashi, Wasagu, Gusau, Tumfafi and Mada in present Zamfara State.

These kingdoms had passed through many distinct stages of social and political transformation. Foremost was the period of the emergence of the pioneer settlements of hamlets, villages and towns based on interdisciplinary relationships, inter-communal co-operation and defence. There was the period of the evolution of the Sarauta system from the Maiunguwa, the Maigari and the Sarki and related institutions. These was the period of the Maguzawa and the Habe dynasties. These was also the period of the evolution and development of various occupational guilds in some specific places across the kingdoms. This gave birth to trade and commerce in goods and services within and outside the areas, a system which produced some important trade routes and the famous trans-Saharan trade. This was the period in which the State attained its highest esteem.

There was the period of the introduction and spread of Islamic religion and learning. The enthusiasm of the inhabitants toward Islam and its preachers as well as the favourable international relations with neighbours facilitated an influx of migrants from the near and the far away empires such as Borno and Songhai into these kingdoms. The Jihad of the 1804's and its aftermath added another dimension to social and political transformation of the area.

There was the period of colonial imposition, the introduction of indirect rule and western education. It was in this period that Katsina and Daura kingdoms were administered as part of Kano and later Zaria provinces. From the late 1960's to late 1980's this area was part of the north-central and then Kaduna State of the Nigerian Federation. Before then, the area had been part of the northern component of the three regional structure of Nigeria; others are western and eastern regions.

The creation of Katsina State added another dimension in the annals of social and political transformation of the area. Since then, the State has witnessed changes in socioeconomic, cultural and political spheres. New Local Government Areas and District Councils have been created. Institutions of higher learning were established in addition to the numerous secondary and tertiary schools. Agencies for the improvement and development of agriculture and centres for information dissemination were established. Other infrastructures such as markets, roads, dams, hospitals etc., were constructed.

The historical developments outlined above have imbued the people of Katsina State with a rich cultural heritage the like of which no other people can boast of in the whole of Hausaland. Perhaps the foremost legacy is the prestigious position of the State as the birth place of the famous *sarauta* system. It was here that the system was evolved, nourished, developed and exported to other areas across Hausaland. It is the first port of call for the famous, Arab scholar Muhammad al-maghili before proceeding to settle in Kano. It is the gateway through which Islam was spread to other parts of Hausaland, with the arrival and activities of the Wangarawa Dyula scholars and merchants in the 14th century. It is the birth place of the famous Islamic scholars Wali Dan Marna and Wali Dan Masani who are today considered patron saints of Katsina State. Through their teaching and writings the two had great influence in the spread of Islam and Islamic knowledge, not only in Katsina but the rest of Hausaland.

Katsina State is the home of the legendary Kusugu well and Gobarau Minaret. It is the birth place of dynamic leaders, brave warriors, intelligent musicians and singers, the likes of Emir Muhammadu Dikko, the legendary Danwaire and Alhaji Muhammadu Shata Katsina. It is the home of some of the Nation's finest soldiers, financial wizards and political heavyweights.

It once served as the best centre of learning in madrasas at Yandoto, Kurmin Dan Ranko, Kahutu, Tsohuwar Kasuwa, Gambarawa, Kusada and Karkarku. The first college in the Northern Region was established in Katsina city in 1921.

Other legacies include norms and values which constitute unique aspects of the people's widely known disposition of courtesy and politeness, popularly referred to as hospitality or 'KARA'. Kara has been associated with Katsina and its inhabitants since antiquity. It is this deposition that entitles Katsina to its current epithet as the 'Home of Heritage and Hospitality.'

Katsina and Daura Kings' lists are given in Table 2.5. Presently, Katsina State consists of thirty-four Local Government Council Areas. These Local Government Areas were carved out from the two emirates as follows;-

Katsina Emirate 29 Local Government Areas

Daura Emirate 5 Local Government Areas.

The territory of each Emirate is divided into districts, village areas and hamlets or wards, headed respectively by District Heads (Hakimai), Village Heads (Magaddai) and Ward Heads (Masu Ungunni). The Emir of Katsina Alhaji (Dr) Abdulmuminu Kabir Usman and Emir of Daura Alhaji Umar Faruk Umar administer these areas and are responsible for the appointment, discipline and removal of Village Heads and of District Heads with the approval of the State Governor in case of the latter. Katsina Emirate comprises 44 Districts and 470 Village Areas, whilst Daura Emirate contains 16 Districts and 136 Village Areas.

Land Area: 24308.40 Square kilometres;

Population (2006 Census)

Male	2,948,279
Female	2,853,305
Total	5,801,584

The breakdown of the population of the 34 local government areas is given in Table 2.7.

Structure Of State Government

There are three Arms of government;-
  (1) Executive Arm headed by the State Governor;
  (2) Legislative Arm - headed by the Speaker of the State Assembly;
  (3) Judiciary - headed by the State Chief Judge.

The Executive Arm

This comprises the Executive Governor; Alhaji Ibrahim Shehu Shema is the current Governor of Katsina State. He appoints Commissioners, Secretary to the State Government, Special Advisors, Special Assistants and other aides to assist him in the administration of the state government. The Commissioners who constitute the State Executive Council are in charge of State Ministries which include the following;-

>   Education;
>   Justice;
>   Agriculture, Natural Resources;
>   Works and Transport;
>   Women Affairs;
>   Commerce, Industry and Tourism;
>   Health;
>   Information and Home Affairs;
>   Social Development, Youth and Sports;
>   Water Resources;
>   Land, Survey and Environment.

The State Civil Service comprises;-

Head of Service;
Permanent Secretaries;

Departmental Directors and their Assistants; who run the day to day affairs of the ministries.

There are also agencies, parastatals which are supervised by the ministries. The civil servants are employees of the state government and not elected officials or political appointees. There are also extra-ministerial departments independent of ministerial control. These include Civil Service Commission, Auditor Generals Office, State Independent Electoral Commission, Local Government Service Commission, Pension Board etc.

The Legislature

Consists of 34 members, one elected to represent a Local Government Area. The principal officers of the legislature are;-

(1) The Speaker who is the presiding officer and his Deputy;
(2) Majority and Minority Leaders;
(3) Chief Whip and other Whips.

The clerk of the House is head of the management and staff of the legislature who serve the various standing and ad hoc committees established by the legislature.

The sergeant at Arms is the custodian of the Mace, a symbol of authority without which the legislature cannot legitimately meet to transact official business.

The Judiciary comprises;-

(1) The State Chief Judge and Judges of the High Court;
(2) The Magistrate Courts.

The Grand Kadi and Judges of Sharia Courts - Upper and Lower Sharia Courts who dispense justice in accordance with the Sharia Law.

As stated above, the Executive arm of government comprises Ministries, Departments and Agencies (MDA's) headed by Commissioners who supervise regular employees of state government such as Permanent Secretaries, Directors-General, Directors and other subordinate staff. The MDAs carry out the day-to-day running of government business in the following areas.

Education

1. There are 2,174 primary schools with a total enrolment of 1,230,023 pupils; 211 junior secondary schools with a total enrolment of 154,228 pupils, 116 senior secondary schools with a total enrolment 98,763 pupils in 2008/09 school year.

Katsina State was at one time one of the Northern States with the lowest male/female pupil ratio in school enrolment. But with the efforts made through the GEP (Girl Education Programme) sponsored by UNICEF and collaboration of state and traditional authorities, the ratio improved considerably. In some local government areas such as Kurfi, the ratio is almost 50:50 male/female pupils.

The state government embarked on massive recruitment of primary and secondary school teachers in order to match this phenomenal increase in the enrolment of school pupils. The number of classrooms was also increased by erecting storey buildings in many primary and secondary schools throughout the state. In addition, new junior secondary schools and girls primary schools were built by the thirty-four local government councils at the direction of state government. The combination of these measures has the effect of improving the teacher/pupil ratio from over hundred pupils per teacher to less than fifty. Katsina is one of the educationally advanced states in the North, if not in the whole country. This is a tremendous improvement in the educational development of the state which at one time was below that of other states, even in the educationally backward North.

The achievements of the State Government in the educational sector are outlined in the recent press brief issued by the Hon. Commissioner of Education which forms Table 2.1.

2. The following tertiary Institutions are located in Katsina State;-

  (a) Hassan Usman Katsina Polytechnic, Katsina;
  (b) Federal College of Education, Katsina;
  (c) Usman Danfodio Institute, Katsina;
  (d) Bala Usman College of Legal and General Studies, Daura;
  (e) Isa Kaita College of Education, Dutsinma;
  (f) School of Basic and Remedial Studies, Funtua;
  (g) Katsina (Islamic) University, Katsina;
  (h) Umaru Musa 'Yar'adua University, Katsina.

Health Care Development

The following health facilities/centres/institutions are located at various parts of Katsina State ;-

1.   Number of Primary Health Units

      (a) Comprehensive health centres   22
      (b) Other primary health centres   100
      (c) Dispensaries   200

2. Number of general hospitals   20
3. Number of specialist hospitals   1
4. Number of health training institutions   4
    (a) School of Health Technology, Kankia;
    (b) School of Health Technology, Daura;
    (c) School of Nursing Katsina;
    (d) School of Health Technology, Malumfashi.
5. Number of Federal Health Institutions
    Federal Medical Centre   1

6. Other Health Facilities   824
    (a) Private   50
    (b) Health Centre   518
    (c) Maternal and Child Health Centre   154
    (d) Health Posts   102

Works, Housing And Transport

During the period 1999 - 2007 Katsina State embarked on construction, rehabilitation of roads in all the three Senatorial Districts of the state. Major arterial roads linking strategic centres of economic activities were constructed. This include the following;-

1.   Katsina - Tsagero - Mani

2. Tama - Charanci - Matazu - Mararrabar Musawa;
3. Charanci - Denye - Kurfi;
4. Faskari - Dandume - Sabuwa;
5. Gidan mutun Daya - Ingawa - Mani - Mashi;
6. Fago - Rijiyar Tsamiya - Dan Nakola;
7. Kankara - Sheme;
8. Malumfashi - Mahuta.

Current Projects Awarded From 2007

1. Construction of Katsina Township Roads Phase V;
2. Construction of Mani - Magami - Gewayau - Dutsi Road;
3. Conversion of township roads to dual carriageway in Dutsinma;
4. Conversion of township roads to dual carriageway and upgrading of Daura Township Roads;
5. Construction of Karfi - Kuringafa - Tsiga - Yarkasuwa Roads;
6. Construction of Kurfi - Batsari Roads;
7. Conversion of township roads dual carriageway in Malumfashi;
8. Construction of Ingawa Township Roads;
9. Construction of Kankara - Ketare - Gora with Malumfashi Spur Road;
10. Construction of New G.R.A Road (Katsina Township Roads Phase VI;
11. Construction of Mashi - Birnin Kuka Road;
12. Construction of Batsari - Jibia Road;
13. Construction of Kankia Township Roads.

Water Resources - Rivers And Dams

Many rivers, brooks and other water courses criss - cross the land mass of Katsina State. Amongst the major rivers are;-

1. River Gada
2. River Bunsuru/Karaduwa
3. River Gagare
4. River Sokoto
5. River Turarni
6. River Tagwai
7. River Sabke.

There are also dams constructed for irrigation farming, water supply to urban, semi-urban and rural population, fish farming, as well as electricity generation. Table 2.2 gives a list of principal/major dams in Katsina State.

Ministry Of Commerce, Industry And Tourism

The creation of Katsina State brought with it the usual increase in the volume of economic and social activities attendant to a new state. Major cash crops produced in the state are millet, guinea-corn, groundnut, cotton, maize, beans, and rice. Katsina State is the largest producer of cotton in Nigeria and livestock production is also a major pre-occupation of people in the State.

The agricultural products of the state provide good raw material base for a variety of industries such as oil and flour milling, textiles and diary products. The largest industrial ventures in the state include Katsina Steel Rolling Company, which produce variety of iron rods, wire of different dimensions etc. Katsina Flour Mills which produces flour, Hamada Carpets, paints and chalk making industries in all the local governments and many more are expected in due course. There are bright prospects for Katsina State to take its rightful place in industrial and commercial activities in the country if its natural resources are properly harnessed for that purpose. Improvement, especially in the infrastructural sector (roads, water, and electricity etc.,) is currently going on in order to achieve this purpose.

Agricultural Produce

The availability of various types of crops cultivated in the state provides the opportunities for the setting up of agro-allied industries. As previously stated, cotton, beans, tomatoes and pepper, groundnut, millet, maize and guinea-corn are raw material for various types of industries. Leather and shoe manufacturing industries are feasible because of the availability in commercial quantity of hide and skin in all the nooks and crannies of the state.

Funtua textiles factory which employs over one thousand workers depends heavily on cotton being produced in Funtua, Bakori, Dandume, Sabuwa, Faskari, Danja, Dutsin-ma, Kurfi, Malumfashi and Kafur local government areas.

The availability of these raw materials offers wide ranging opportunities for setting up of more commercial and industrial ventures in the state.

The two oil mills situated in Katsina and Funtua depend on groundnut and cotton seed for their raw material requirements.

Mineral Resources

Katsina State is blessed with abundant mineral resources that could be tapped for industrial growth. Prominent amongst these include; - Lead, Iron Oxide, Gold, Ore, Manganese, Kaolin, Silica Sands, Fire Clay, Ball Clay, Asbestos, Feldspars, Mica, Serpentine, Gemstones, Precious stones etc.

The availability of Kaolin deposits in various locations in the state has led to the establishment of the Kankara Pharmaceutical Kaolin Factory and Katsina Chalk and Paint factories. Table 2.3 gives a list of major industries in Katsina State.

Military And Civilian Administrations From 1987 To Date (2009)

Since its creation on September 27, 1987 Katsina State has had ten administrations headed by the following governors/administrators;-

(1) First military administration

Governor: Colonel Abdullahi Sarki Mjukhtar from September 1987 to July 1988.

(2) Second military administration
Governor: Colonel Laurence A. Onoja from July 1988 to 1990.

(3) Third military administration
Governor: Colonel John Yahaya Madaki, from July 1990 - 1992.

(4) First civilian administration
Governor: Alhaji Sa'idu Barda from January 1992 to

November 1993.
(5) Fourth military administration
Governor: Navy Captain E.A Acholono from 1993 to 1996.
(6) Fifth military administration
Governor: Colonel S.B Chama from 1996 to 1998.
(7) Sixth military administration
Governor: Colonel J.I Akagege from 1998 to 1999.
(8) Second and third civilian administrations
Governor: Alhaji Umaru Musa Yar adua from 29th May 1999 to 29th May 2003 and from 29th May 2003 to 29th May 2007.
(9) Fourth civilian adminstration
Governor: Alhaji Ibrahim Shehu Shema from 29th May 2007 to date 2009.

Since its creation in 1987, Katsina State has witnessed tremendous growth in all fields of human endeavour, especially in the execution of development projects. The tempo of progress accelerated from 1999 with the inception of democratic governance after almost twelve years of military rule (1987 to 1999). In particular the education, health, housing and road development sectors witnessed tremendous growth. The state government built hundreds of housing units at Goriba Housing Estate in Katsina city and has also embarked on construction of five hundred housing units of various sizes. The government also directed each of the thirty-four local governments to build thirty houses at the local government headquarters. Most of these projects have been completed or are on the verge of being so.

The number of educational institutions at primary, secondary and tertiary levels multiplied and several were upgraded. The increase in school enrolment at all levels was phenomenal. Similarly, many roads were constructed and or rehabilitated and other infrastructures were also improved. Katsina State equals, if not surpassed many states in the federation and this is confirmed by several awards given to it by the Federal Government, the latest being the prize it won on its accomplishments in the Universal Basic Education Programme. The laudable development programmes initiated by its former governor Alhaji Umaru Yar adua between 1999 and 2007 has continued under the present governor, Alhaji Ibrahim Shehu Shema whose achievements in the last two years (2007 - 2009) are commendable and worthy of emulation by other states in Nigeria.

Katsina State Government under Governor Umaru Musa Yar adua initiated, executed and completed the following gigantic projects within record time.

(1) State Secretariat building at Dandagoro which was abandoned by previous regimes was resuscitated, completed and commissioned by the Yar adua administration;

(2) State High Court building complex on Katsina - Daura road;

(3) Umaru Musa Yar adua University initiated completed, commissioned and occupied within less than three years, thanks to the efforts made by the Ibrahim Shehu Shema administration toward the realization of the objectives of the initiator of the project. These elegant edifices are comparable to similar buildings executed elsewhere in the country. They can be referred to as the Three Wonders of Katsina State development projects.

Figure 2.1: Map of Katsina State

(4) Katsina Airport was upgraded to international airport and for the first time intending pilgrims from Katsina State were airlifted to and from the Holy land from the new airport in 2007. Before that date pilgrims from

Katsina State had to travel to Kano in buses to be airlifted to Saudi Arabia, with all the dangers that such journey entailed.

Katsina The Great Province

Katsina State and its indigenes had set several achievement records at regional and national levels. Many of such achievements would certainly escape the mind, but an attempt is hereby made to list as many as possible

1. The first college to be built in Northern Nigeria was the Katsina College, built in 1921 and commissioned in 1922.

2. The first Northerner to become a Permanent Secretary in the regional civil service was late Alhaji Ahmadu Kumasi in 1960.

3. The first Hausa to become an Army General was General Hassan Usman Katsina in 1973.

4. The first Northerner to hold a political office under a military dispensation was General Hassan Usman Katsina who became the Governor of Northern Nigeria in 1966.

5. The first Northerner to become a Veterinary Doctor was late Alhaji (Dr) Abu Mawashi in 1951.

6. The first international radio broadcaster was Alhaji Isa Kaita, Wazirin Katsina, who along with Alhaji Bello Dandago from Kano served the BBC, Accra station in 1941.

7. The first Pharmacy school in Northern Nigeria (called Medical Class) was built in Katsina in 1927.

8. The first Northerners to become chattered accountants were Alhaji (Dr.) Hamza Zayyad Rafindadi (Wazirin Katsina) and Alhaji Umar Idris Dandamu in 1962.

9. The first Emir in Nigeria to travel officially to England was late Sarkin Katsina Muhammad Dikko in 1921.

10. The longest reigning Emir in modern times was late Sarkin Daura Abdul-Rahman who ruled from 1911 to 1966 (fifty-five years).

11. The first modern day Emir to perform the Holy Pilgrimage (Hajj) was late Sarkin Katsina Muhammad Dikko in 1921.

12. The first Northerners to become lawyers were Justice Muhammadu Bello and Justice Mamman Nasir in 1955.

13. The first Northerner to become Minister of Justice was Justice Mamman Nasir (Galadiman Katsina) in 1960.

14. The first Northerner to become Chief Justice of Nigeria was Justice Muhammadu Bello in 1987.

15. The first Northerner to become a Civil Engineer was Engineer Mahmud Urwatu Armaya'u in 1953.

16. The first female Hausa to become a Doctor was Dr. Halima Yalwa in 1976.

17. The first Nigerian Nurse to receive a National Honour was late Alhaji Mande of Katsina General Hospital fame in 1963.

18. The youngest Nigeria to be appointed an Ambassador was late Ambassador Iro Ladan Baki who served in the Netherlands from 1987 at the age of 34 years.

19. The first Traditional Musician to receive a National Honour and to be awarded a Doctorate Degree was Dr. Alhaji Mamman Shata Katsina.

20. The first Treasury to be established in Northern Nigeria was at Katsina near the Emir's Palace in 1906.

21. The first Polo Club in Northern Nigeria was established in Katsina in 1921.

22. The first Minister to move from Lagos to the new Federal Capital, Abuja, was Alhaji Samaila Mamman, the Minister of Commerce in 1987.

23. The best Polo team in Nigeria was that led by late Sir Usman Nagogo with a combined handicap of plus (+) 20.

24. The most famous sports gallery in Nigeria is that at the Emirs Palace Katsina with over 500 trophies.

25. The most famous Well in Nigeria is the Kusugu Well in Daura dug over 1,100 years ago.

26. The best Polo player ever produced in Nigeria was late Sir Usman Nagogo with a plus (+) 7 handicap. He was also the best Nigerian Horse Racing Jockey with 51 gold and hundreds of Silver winnings.

27. The Province with the highest number of ministerial appointments in the first Republic was Katsina Province. No other province ever produced up to seven Ministers at the same time, except Katsina (1964-

1966). In addition, the Emir of Katsina was the first Northerner to be appointed a Federal Minister in 1952.

28. The first Agricultural Research Centre in Northern Nigeria was the Cotton Improvement Centre at Daudawa near Funtua established in 1920 and later moved to Ahmadu Bello University at Samaru, Zaria.

29. The first Hausa to become the Nigerian Inspector General of Police was Alhaji M.D. Yusuf in 1975.

30. The first Hausaland Kings were the grandchildren of Bayjidda who ruled the seven Hausa states around 990 AD.

31. The first Palace to be built in Hausaland was of Queen Daurama in Daura which is over 1,200 years old.

32. The first community owned university in Nigeria is the Katsina Islamic University under a non-governmental organisation, the Katsina Islamic Foundation. Its construction started in November 1999.

33. The first veterinary centre in Northern Nigeria was built at Modoji village (present Government House vicinity) Katsina in 1919.

34. The most famous Hausaland equivalent of today's university was the Gobarau Islamic Centre established in 1493 AD and affiliated to the famous Sankore University at Timbuktu.

Ministry Of Education Katsina State

Katsina State Government's Giant Strides In The Development Of Education

Preamble

Education as the bedrock upon which all other developmental policies and programmes are based and, indeed, is the instrument for complete national renaissance. This administration inherited reinvigorated system of education whose rehabilitation was begun by the past administration. The poor state of infrastructure inherited then, lack of instructional material and lack of teachers etc., had all been attacked head on by the past administration and Alhaji Ibrahim Shehu Shema administration followed suit.

The state government, through the Ministry of Education, is currently embarking upon positive efforts which have improved the quality of education that the children in the state are now receiving. The Ministry has continued to ensure that the business of education is run along the line of the objectives enumerated in the National Policy on Education, but tailored to the specific educational and socio-economic needs the state

2.0 Objectives Of The Ministry

The objectives of the ministry include reviewing and streamlining of some initiatives with a view to achieving total arrest of the falling standard of education in the state.

3.0 Mission/Vision

The mission/vision of the ministry entails a systematic and gradual implementation of some cardinal principles aimed at total resuscitation of the education sector in order to regain the sector's lost glory by the year 2015, in line with the principles of the Millennium Development Goals.

In addition, the under-listed are parastatals under supervision of the ministry:

    a) State Universal Basic Education Board (SUBEB)

    b) Science and Technical Education Board (STEB)

    c) Agency for Mass Education (AME)

    d) Teachers' Service Board (TSB)

    e) Mathematical Improvement Project (MIP)

The Government of Katsina State under the administration of Alhaji Ibrahim Shehu Shema has recorded great achievement in the education sector for the past two years, this can evidently be envisaged as to the colossus sum of finances devoted to resuscitate the lost glory of educational position of the State.

No wonder, Alhaji Ibrahim Shehu Shema's regime devoted all its resources towards the following:

    A) Provision access to as many greater populations of the youth to education through an expansion of the existing schools and establishment of new ones (as could be seen in the attached synopsis).

    B) Provision of free education from primary to secondary school, and the payment of running cost and even national and international examination fees for all students in the state public and community secondary schools. (These details are also provided in the synopsis).

C) Provision of other infrastructural facilities for learning and teaching in schools, such as classroom furniture, laboratory equipment and material, technical and ICT equipment and connectivity etc.

D) Capacity building of the existing and newly recruited teachers, in all areas of study.

E) Recruitment of more teachers. Incentive for the retention of the teachers, which include payment of rent subsidy allowance to all teachers, in respective of those living in the staff quarters.

F) Free accommodation to all teachers residing in government quarters in the state secondary schools, and provision of more quarters under the expansion programme and in the newly established secondary schools.

All these measures are put in place to provide conducive atmosphere to cope with ever growing enrolment of students in our schools.

Table 2.1: Educational Development In Katsina State

KATSINA STATE MINISTRY OF EDUCATION

S/NO	ITEM OF EXPENDITURE	AMOUNT	PERIOD
1.	Payment of WASSCE/NECON/NABTEB/NBAIS fees for all candidates in Katsina State Government Post Primary Institutions.	N140,505,800.oo	2008 May/June/ July Exams
2.	Schools Running cost in place of school fees charged by Principals of Schools, N800 per boarding student per session and N570 per day student per session.	N160,688,487.67k	2nd and 3rd terms of 2007/08 session
3.	Schools running cost in place of school fees charged by Principals of schools. N800 per boarding student per session and N570 per day student per session.	N149,170,146.67k	1st, 2nd, 3rd term of 2008/09 session
4.	First Aid kits to secondary schools in the state	N6,520,000.oo	In 2008
5.	On going recruitment of 3000 teachers to provide the much needed manpower in our schools as part of short and medium term scheme.	N500,000,000.oo	2009
6.	Establishment of 103 new junior secondary schools in collaboration with the Local Government Councils in the state.	N6,935,631,492.24k	2006 – 2008
7.	Construction of JAMB office, already handed over to the State Coordinator.	N42,000,000.oo N8,700,000.oo	2008
8.	100% upward review of feeding allowances paid to the principals of Boarding secondary schools in the state. Already budgetary provision has been made to reflect the upward review.	N505,168,000.oo	2009
9.	Teachers training NERDC for 9 – Basic year curriculum implementation.	N4,900,000.oo	2009

10.	Rehabilitation for the installation of 100 units computers in 10 schools and Training of 100 teachers in collaboration with USPF/Dialogue Global Links Ltd	N26,252,625.00	2009
11.	Train the trainers workshop for Headmasters in the use of new Continuous Assessment Instruments	N896,000.00	Jan. 2008
12.	Production of Teaching Scheme for Junior Secondary Schools	N3,500,000.00	2008
13.	Production of Continues Assessment dossiers for Senior and Junior Secondary Schools	N7,500,000.00	2008
14.	157 teachers attended diagnostic workshop on English language		
15.	80 teachers attended computer training;		
16.	The following number of teachers attended Mathematics/Science Workshops in different places: (a)7 in Sokoto; (b)10 in Kano;(c)30 in FCE Katsina 47 teachers benefited		
17.	Training of Inspectors towards effective school supervision 120 Inspectors		
18.	Workshop on School Management and Leadership skills for Principal and vice Principals	337 Principals 663 Vice Principals	
19.	Procurement of the new 9 year Basic Education curriculum	N2,975,570.00	2008
20.	Training of teachers on the usage of the new 9 year Basic Education curriculum	N4,900,000.00	2008
21.	Conduct Of Junior Secondary Schools Certificate Examination (JSSCE)	N20,000,000.00	2008
22.	Junior Engineers Technicians and Scientists (JETS) quiz competition at Zonal and State levels.	N250,000.00	2008
23.	Participation in the National Junior Engineers Technicians and Scientists (JETS quiz competition at the North West Zonal chapter.	N120,000.00	2008
24.	Production and binding of booklets of junior secondary schools certificate examination (jssce) results, according to the seven educational zones in the State	N1,500,000.00	2008

25.	Exhibition of Instructional materials	N370,000.00	2008
26.	**SUDAN**	N200,569,070.00	2008
a.	Money spent on students on course to Sudan		
b.	Number of students involved is 111		
c.	i)ii)iii)iv)v)Universities involves are: International University of Africa Ahfad University for Women Omdruman Islamic University Al-Needlain University Khartoum Sudan University of Science and Technology Khartoum International Institute for Arabic Language		
d.	i)ii)iii)iv)v)vi) SUMMARY OF COURSES Medicines – 10 Pharmacy – 08 Nursing – 04PGD in Arabic Editing and publishing – 15Diploma in Arabic and Computer programming – 57 Diploma in Arabic Calligraphy – 17		
27.	**EQUIPMENT**		
a.	Fire fighting equipment for Secondary Schools	N17,232,750.00	2009
b.	First Aid Kits	N6,520,000.00	2008
c.	Transportation of students on Exchange programme by KTSTA	10,329,850.00 N2,728,300.00	20082009 2007/
d.	Computer supplied and maintenance	N2,000,000.00	2009
28.	**Instructional Materials**		
a.	Customize textbooks	N13,892,957.00	2008
b.	Curriculum books 309 sets	N2,975,570.00	
c.	C.A. Booklets (25,000) copies	N7,500.000.00	2008
29.	**Science & Technical Education Board**		
a.	Science Equipment supplied to schools	N80,000,000.00	2007/2008
b.	Computers supplied	N5,000,000.00	2007/2008
c.	Extension programme of final year students	N3,500.000.00	2007/2008
d.	Purchase of Technical Equipment to schools	N20,180,000.00	2008/2009
e.	Extension programme of final year students	N4,000,000.00	2008/2009
f.	Purchase of addition 5 No luxurious pilot school buses	N92,000.000.00	2008
30.	**State Universal Basic Education Board**		
a.	Motorcycle loan scheme to teachers	N280,000.000.00 N280,000.000.00	20072008
b.	Overhead costs given to LGEA's at 5% of total emoluments of each Local Government		
c.	Senior Staff Promotion from GL.07 and above in the LGEA's and SUBEB 2,860 staff 2,560 staff		20072008
d.	Instructional materials state funds	N117,067.670.00	2007-2008
e.	UBE Instructional Materials	N200,299,881.40	2007
f.	Additional Classrooms for GEP schools in 6 GEP LGEA's	N35,129,178.50 N30,289,140.00	20072008

h.	Construction and extension of story building on existing ones at Tsiga, Danja, Mani, Kaura Abdulkadir, Nuhu, Dallaje, Faskari Primary Schools as well as procurement of 12,240 units of pupils desks and chairs (metal)	N535,353,246.01	2007
g.	Construction and extension of story building in Na-Alhaji Mashi, Kafur Usman Liman and Muh'd Dikko Primary Schools (UBEC intervention funds projects)	N518,493,867.70	2008
i	Direct efforts of the State Government in staff training in-service, NCE DLS, Diploma in Arabic/ Islamic Studies DLS, Long Vocational Training and Curriculum Development for a total number of 10,521 staff	N112,947,860.66	2007 - date
j.	Katisna State Counterpart funding	N632,364,864.00 N832,432,432.00 N480,613,194.00	20072008 2009
31.	Expansion and Rehabilitation of Secondary Schools through the provision of additional classroom blocks, well equipped laboratories, libraries, junior and senior staff quarters, NYSC lodge, computer centers, sick bays, supply of furniture, science materials and reference text books.	N3,877,916,350	2005
32.	Expansion and rehabilitation of additional junior and senior secondary schools as well as the establishment of 7 new turn key junior secondary schools, with 4 blocks of three classrooms, admin block, multipurpose laboratory and workshop in each school.	N4,142,140,715	2006
33.	Expansion and Rehabilitation of Secondary Schools through the provision of additional classroom blocks, well equipped laboratories, libraries, junior and senior staff quarters, NYSC lodge, and computer centers, and sick bays, supply of furniture, science materials and references text books. This is on going.	N4,310,579,465	2007
34.	Rehabilitation and expansion of additional existing senior and junior secondary schools in the state.	N5,952,846,372	2008
35.	Earmarked huge sum of money for capital projects including the completion and consolidation of the ERC and the Seven Zonal Offices.	N4,575,432,432	2009
36.	The schools mass transit scheme has greatly improved the attendance to school of the Girls, and has brought subsidy to the transportation of their wards to school		
37.	Workshop for teachers towards effective teaching of social studies and other related subjects.	400 teachers	

			benefited	2008
	Workshop for newly recruited teacher		516 teachers benefited	2008
38.	Purchase of science, Technical and Home Economics equipments and materials		N50,000.000.00	2007
39	Procurement of customized books by the Mathematical Improvement Project and distributed to Secondary Schools in the State		N13,334,250.00	2008
40.	Two students in the state qualified for the National Olympaid of the NMC			Oct. 2008

39

Table 2.2: List of Existing Principal/Major Dams in Katsina State

KASTINA STATE GOVERNMENT
MINISTRY OF WATER RESOURCES

S/N	Name of Reservoir	Capacity of (M^3)	Approx. Height(M)	Name of River	Location of Scheme
1	Ajiwa	22 x 10^6	12.0	Tagwai River Valley	Ajiwa
2	Zobe	177 x 10^6	18.5	Bunsuru River Valley	Dustinma
3	Gwaigwaye	7.2 x 10^6	12.0	Sokoto River Valley	Funtua
4	Turo	6.3 x 10^6	12.0	Turami River Valley	Malumfashi
5	Jibia	142 x 10^6	21.3	Gada River Valley	Jibia
6	Sabke	31.6 x 10^6	12.5	Sabke River Valley	Maiaduwa
7	Dustinma	2.5 x 10^6	7.5	River Bunsuru Tribulary	Dustinma
8	Mairuwa	3.5 x 10^6	7.0	River Sokoto Tributary	Dicke/Funtua

Total Capacity 392.1 x 10^6

List of Urban water supply Schemes in the State

S/N	Name of Scheme	Benefitting community	Local Govt.	Qty Supplied
1	Katsina Water Supply	Katsina and Environ	Katsina	50,000M^3/ day
2	Daura Water Supply	Daura and Environ.	Daura	7,000M^3/day
3	Funtua Water Supply	Funtua and Environ.	Funtua	18,000M^3 / day
4.	Malumfashi Water Supply	Malumfashi and Environ.	Malumfashi	4,500M^3/day
5	Dutsinma Water Supply	Dutsinma and Environ.	Dutsinma	3,500M$^"$/day
6	Jibia Water Supply	Jibia and Environ.	Jibia	6,000M^3/ day
	TOTAL			89,000M^3/day

List of Semi Urban Water Supply Schemes in the State

S/N	NAME OF SCHEME	BENEFITING COMMUNITY	LOCAL GOVT INVOLVED	NO. OF BOREHOLE
1.	Batsari Semi-urban scheme	Batsari town	Batsari	189 M^3/day
2.	Wagini Small town scheme	Wagini	Batsari	539,45 M^3/day
3.	Wagini Small town scheme	Wagini	Batsari	539.45 M^3/day
4.	Zango Semi-urban scheme	Zango	Zango	673.4 M^3/day
5.	Dutsi Semi-Urban scheme	Dutsi	Dutsi	436.3 M^3/day
6.	Maiadua Semi-urban scheme	Maiadua	Maiadua	648 M^3 per day
7.	Mani Semi-urban scheme	Mani	Mani	980 M^3/day
8.	Doro Small town scheme	Doro	Bindawa	162 M^3/day
9.	Bindawa Semi-urban scheme	Bindawa	Bindawa	467.6 M^3/day
10.	Ingawa Semi-urban scheme	Ingawa	Ingawa	290 M^3/day
11.	Kankia Semi-urban scheme	Kankia	Kankia	334.8 M^3/day
12.	Dankama Semi-urban scheme	Dankama	Kaita	1566 M^3/day
13.	Charanci Semi-urban scheme	Charanci	Charanci	340 M^3/day
14.	Radda small town scheme	Radda	Charanci	164.2 M^3/day
15.	Jikamshi Semi-urban scheme	Jikamshi	Musawa	297 M^3/day
16.	Musawa Semi-urban scheme	Musawa	Musawa	405 M^3/day
17.	Matazu Semi-urban scheme	Matazu	Matazu	243 M^3/day
18.	Kankara Semi-urban scheme	Kankara	Kankara	480.6 M^3/day
19.	Kafur Semi-urban scheme	Kafur	Kafur	162 M^3/day
21.	Kurfi Semi-urban scheme	Kurfi	Kurfi	324 M^3/day

22	Faskari Semi-urban scheme	Faskari	Faskari	594 M³ /day
23	Dandume Semi-urban scheme	Dandume	Dandume	451.9 M³ / day
24	Danja Semi-urban scheme	Danja	Danja	286.2 M³ / day
25	Sabuwa Semi-urban scheme	Sabuwa	Sabuwa	640.9 M³ /day
26	Rimi Semi-urban scheme	Rimi	Rimi	394.2 M³ / day
27	Danmusa Small town scheme	Danmusa	Danmusa	349.4 M³ / day
	TOTAL			**12,444.6 M³ / day**

Table 2.3: Major Industries in Katsina State

S/NO	NAME OF ESTABLISHMENT	LOCATION	NATURE OF BUSINESS
1.	Katsina Steel Rolling Company limited Katsina	KM 1 IBB Way Katsina	Wire Rods, Plan and Robbing Boards, Wire Drawn etc.
2	Saulawa Machines Fabrication Company Ltd Katsina	W.T.C Road Katsina	Bolt & Bute Metal Fabrication Concrete Block
3	M/Fashi Wood/Metal Construction Company Malumfashi	No. 131 Kano Road Malumfashi	Wood/Metal construction
4	Hamada Carpel Limited Katsina	W.T.C Road Katsina	Turning Carpet Katsina
5	Funtua Textiles Limited Funtua	Sokoto Road, Funtua	Roller Cloth, Bed Sheets etc
6	Shema Industries Limited Dutsinma	Hospital Road Dutsinma	Plastic products fitting
7	Kaita Brothers Limited Katsina	KM 9 Kano Road, Katsina Sabon Layi, Katsina	Candle pomade metal Toilet paper
8	Alheri Shoe Factory Ltd, Katsina.	No. 42 Sabuwa, Funtua	Shoes, Bags & Seat covers.
9	Mailla Agric & Food Processing Company Ltd, Funtua	No. 89 IBB Way, Katsina Nagogo Road, Katsina Katsina Road, Funtua.	Food Processing
10	Nakowa Bakery Limited, Katsina	Goron Gida, Katsina	Bread and Cakes etc
11	Wapa Yoghurts	KT 1 IBB Way, Katsina	Yoghurt & Orange Juice
12	Funtua Cotton Seed Crushing Company Ltd Funtua	IBB Way, Katsina	Cooking Oil, Cakes, Chicken feeds.
13	Sahel Enterprises Limited	Kano Road	Food and Beverage
14	Katsina Oil Mill Limited, Katsina	Malumfashi	Groundnut Oil, Cooking Oil, G/nut Cakes
15	Nur Enterprises	Sokoto Road, Funtua	Food Processing
16	Alheri Shoe Factory Ltd, Katsina	Ballon Bye-pess Funtua. Zaria Road Funtua	Furniture
17	Funtua Bottling Company Ulrited Funtua	Kankara Mashi-Mani Road Mashi	Soft Drinks
18	Northern Dairies Ltd		Whole Mil etc
19	Funtua Burnt Bricks Ltd	Dutsinma	Burnt Bricks
20	Kankara Kaolin Processing Company	Kankara	Query and Refinishing Kaolin
21	Alh. Y. Usman & Son Company Ltd Mashi	M/Karankara Malumfashi	Laundry Soap Bar Soap
22	Dustinma Tannery	Funtua	Tannery Sina
23	Kankara Ginnery '	Dustinma Road	Ginnery
24	Mararraba Ginnery	Katsina	Ginenry
25	Mararraba Ginnery	Katsina	Ginnery
26	Funtua Cotton Ginnery	Funtua	Ginnery
27	Katsina Flour Mills	Malumfashi	Flour
28	Glorious- Modern Furniture		Furniture
29	Katsina Industrial Mineral deposits		Processing
30	Malumfashi Oil Mill		Cotton Seed Oil

43

Table 2.4: Names and Dates of Dynasties in Katsina

SARAKUNAN KATSINA DAGA FARKO ZUWA YANZU

S/NO	SUNA	LOKACI
1	Kumayau	-
2	Runba-Runba	-
3	Batare –tare	-
4	Korau	-
5	Jin Narata	-
6	Yanka Tsari	-
7	Jidda Yaki (Sanau)	-
8	Sarkin Katsina Muhammadu Korau	1348-1398
9	Sarkin Katsian Usman Maje	1398-1405
10	Sarkin Katsina Ibrahim Soro	1405-1408
11	Sarkin Katsina Marubuci	1408-1426
12	Sarkin Katsina Muhammadu Turare	1426-1436
13	Sarkin Katsian Ali Murabus	1436-1462
14	Sarkin Katsina Ali Karya Giwa	1462-1475
15	Sarkin Katsina Usman Tsaga Rana 1	14-75-1525
16	Sarkin Katsina Usman Damisa Gudu 1	1525-1531
17	Sarkin Katsina Ibrahim Maje	1531-1599
18	Sarkin Katsina Malam Yusuf	1599-1613
19	Sarkin Katsina Abdulkadir	1613-1615
20	Sarkin Katsina Ashafa	1615
21	Sarkin Katsina Gabdo	1615-1625
22	Sarkin Katsina Muhammadu Wari	1625-1637
23	Sarkin Katina Muhammadu Tsaga Rana	1637-1649
24	Sarkin Katsina Maikaraye	1649-1660
25	Sarkin Katsina Suleiman	1660-1673
26	Sarkin Katsina Usman Tsaga Rana II	1673-1692
27	Sarkin Katsina Toyariru	1692-1705
28	Sarkin Katsina Yanja Tsari	1705-1708
29	Sarkin Katsina Usman Yara	1708-1740
30	Sarkin Katsina Jan Hazo	1740-1751
31	Sarkin Katsina Tsaga Rana	1751-1764
32	Sarkin Katsina Mohammadu Kayiba	1764-1771
33	Sarkin Katsina Karya Giwa	1771-1788
34	Sarkin Katsina Giwa Agwaragi	1788-1802
35	Sarkin Katsina Gozo	1802-18-4
36	Sarkin Katsina Bawa dan Giwa	18-4-1805
37	Sarkin Katsina Mud'd Maremawa	1805-1806
38	Sarkin Katsina Magajin Haladu	1806-1807
39	Sarkin Katsina Umarum Dallaje	1807-1835
40	Sarkin Katsina Muhammadu Bello	1835-1844
41	Sarkin Katsina Saddiku Dan Umaru	1844-1869
42	Sarkin Katsina Ahmadu Rufa 'I (Dan Umarun Dallaje)	1869

43	Sarkin Katsina Ibrahim dan Muh'd Bello	1869-1882
44	Sarkin Katsina Musa Dan Umarun Dallaje	1882-1887
45	Sarkin Katsina Abubakar Dan Ibrahim	1887-1905
46	Sarkin Katsina Yero Dan Musa	1905-1906
47	Sarkin Katsina Muhammadu Dikko	1906-1944
48	Sarkin Katsina Usman Nagogo	1944-1981
49	Sarkin Katsina Muh'd Kabir Usman (Dan Usmanu Nagogo)	1981-2008
50	Sarkin Katsina Abdulmumini Kabir Usman	2008-Date

*Dankousou and Charanchi Katsina Dakin

Table 2.5: List of Kings and Queens of Daura

LIST OF THE QUEENS AND KINGS OF DAURA

S/NO	NAME	YEAR	MONTH	DAYS
1.	Kufuru	-	-	-
2.	Gino	-	-	-
3.	Yakumo	-	-	-
4,	Yakunya	-	-	-
5.	Walzamu	-	-	-
6.	Yanbamu	-	-	-
7.	Gizirgizir	-	-	-
8.	Innagari	-	-	-
9.	Daura (Daura)	150	-	-
10.	Gamata (Hamata)	-	-	-
11.	Shata	-	-	-
12.	Batatume (Batatuma)	-	-	-
13.	Sandamata (Saidamata)	-	-	-
14.	Jamata	-	-	-
15.	Hamata	-	-	-
16.	Zama	-	-	-
17	Shawata	-	-	-

LIST OF THE QUEENS AND KINGS OF DAURA

S/NO	NAME	YEAR	MONTH	DAYS
1.	Abayajidda (Sarki)	150	-	-
2.	Bawo	90	3	7
3.	Gazaura	110	-	-
4.	Gakurna	71	-	2
5	Jaaku (Jaku)	80	1	-
6	Jaketake	50	-	10
7	Yakama (Yakuma)	201	-	-
8	Jaka	30	-	-
9	Ada Hamta (Ada Hamata)	600	-	4
10	Ada Jabu (Ada Jabau)	20	-	-
11	Dagamu (Daguma)	8	5	-
12	Ada Yaki	106	-	-
13	Hamdogu (Hamdau)	210	4	1
14	Yabau	-	-	10
15	Naji	7	-	-
16	Gani	33	-	-
17	Wake	15	-	-
18	Kamutu	40	-	-
19	Rigo	1	-	-
20	Gaga	50	-	-
21	Jabu (Jabau)	1	8	-
22	Zammau	4	-	1
23	Shashimi (Shashima)	9	-	-
24	Ada Inda	-	-	½
25	Doguma (Daguma)	109	-	-
26	Ada Gamu (Ada Gamau)	30	-	-
27	Ada Sunguma	-	7	-
28	Shafau (Sahkau)	5	-	-
29	Ada Sabau	8	-	-
30	Ada Doki	99	-	-
31	Nagama	6	-	-
32	Ada Kube	60	-	-
33	Hamama (Hammau)	6	-	-
34	Dagajirau (Dagajarau)	30	6	-
35	Kamu	-	-	3
36	Ada Guguwa	40	-	-
37	Hamida	-	-	10
38	Abdu Kawo	9	-	-
39	Nagama	6	-	-
40	Hamatari	Not known	Not known	Not known
41	Rifau (Rufa;i)	80	-	-
42	Hazo (hazo Allah Sarki)	-	-	-
43	Dango	-	-	-
44	Bawan Allah	-	-	-
45	Kalifa	-	-	-
46	Tsofo	-	-	-

S/NO	NAME	YEAR	MONTH	DAYS
47	Jiro	-	-	-
48	Sarkin Gwari Abdu	-	-	-
49	Lukudi (Brother of 48)	30	-	-
50	Nuhu (son of 48)	15	-	-
51	Mahamman (Son of 48)	3	3	-
52	Haruna (Son of 49)	6	6	-
53	Dan Aro (Son of 48)	6	7	-
54	Sulemanu (Son of 53)	2	-	-
55	Yusufu (Son of 49)	5	-	(6 yrs)
56	Tafida (Son of 50)	20	8	-
57	Malam Musa (Son of 50)	7	5	-
58	Abdurrahman (Son of 57)	Appointed in 1912 – 1966		-
59	Muhammadu Bashar	1966 – 2007		
60	Umar Farouk Umar	2007 – Date		

Table 2.6: Daura Fulani King List

DAURA FULANI KING LIST

S/NO	NAME	YEAR	MONTH	DAYS
1.	Mal. Isyaku	1806-1830		
2.	Yusufu	1830-1836		
3.	Muhamman Sani	1837	8	
4.	Zubairu	1838		
5.	Muhamman Bello	1838-1868	3	
6.	Muhamman Altine	1868-1876		
7.	Muhamman Maigardo	1876-1906	4	
8.	Magajiya Murnai	1906		
9.	Bunturawa Sogiji	1906		9

Table 2.7: Result of Katsina Population Census of 2006

KATSINA = POPULATION 2006 CENSUS

LGA	Both Sexes	Male	Female
Bakori	149,516	72,714	76,802
Batagarawa	189,059	96,693	92,366
Batsari	207,874	104,279	103,595
Baure	202,941	102,127	100,814
Bindawa	151,002	76,925	74,077
Charanchi	136,989	70,040	66,949
Dan Musa	113,190	58,031	55,159
Dandume	145,323	74,222	71,101
Danja	125,481	63,663	61,818
Daura	224,884	115,576	109,308
Dutsi	120,902	61,430	59,472
Dustin-Ma	169,829	88,202	81,627
Faskari	194,400	97,963	96,437
Funtua	225,156	117,789	107,367
Ingawa	169,148	86,061	83,087
Jibia	167,435	85,149	82,286
Kafur	209,360	104,620	104,740
Kaita	182,405	93,190	89,215
Kankara	243,259	121,815	121,444
Kankia	151,395	77,061	74,334
Katsina	518,132	168,906	149,226
Kurfi	116,700	59,021	57,679
Kusada	98,348	50,930	47,418
Mai'adua	201,800	103,107	98,693
Malumfashi	182,891	92,420	90,471
Mani	176,301	88,007	88,294
Mashi	171,070	84,105	86,965
Matazu	113,814	57,587	56,227
Musawa	170,006	85,788	84,218
Rimi	154,092	77,059	77,033
Sabuwa	140,679	72,106	68,573
Safana	185,207	93,410	91,797
Sandamu	136,944	68,512	68,432
Zango	156,052	79,771	76,281
Katsina State	**5,801,584**	**2,948,279**	**2,853,305**

CHAPTER 3

Know your Country – Nigeria

Brief History

In its earliest usage, the name 'Nigeria' was intended to be applied to the northern parts of the country, in order to distinguish those parts from the British colony of Lagos and Niger Coast Protectorate. In a letter to the Times of London (Newspaper) of 8th January 1897, Flora Shaw, the wife of Frederick Lugard, suggested the name 'Nigeria' as a "Shorter title for the agglomeration of Pagan and Mohammedan states which have been brought by the exertions of the Royal Niger Company within the confines of a British protectorate, and thus need for the first time in their history to be described as an entity by some general name (which may serve to differentiate them equally from the British Colony of Lagos and the Niger Protectorate on the coast or from the French.)

Although Flora Shaw's suggestion of a name for the new Colonial entity north of the Niger Coast Protectorate and the Colony and Protectorate of Lagos came to be accepted, its application was made broader. On 1st January 1900, the British Government proclaimed the existence of two new colonial entities, namely, the Protectorate of Northern Nigeria and the Protectorate of Southern Nigeria, along side, but distinct from Colony and Protectorate of Lagos. This act involved the first of a series of three amalgamations which, by 1914, had produced a single colonial entity known as the Colony and Protectorate of Nigeria.

Source - Paper presented by Late Dr. Bala Usman at a national workshop organised by Arewa House, Kaduna in 1994.

The earliest traces of human habitation in what is now Nigeria have been found by 3,000 B.C on the northern plateaux where it is believed agriculture was already being practiced. Between 500 B.C and A.D 200 the Nok culture flourished; it is named after the plateau village where the first of several terra cotta sculptures were discovered. Following the major West African population movements of the first millennium of the Christian era, the ethnographic pattern of Nigeria started to stabilize, with the rise of the mediaeval empires of Ghana, Mali, Songhai and Kanem — Bornu.

The fourteenth and fifteenth centuries saw the rise of the Hausa city states of Katsina, Kano, Gobir, Zaria, etc in the North as well as the appearance of Nupe and Kwararafa kingdoms in the middle belt area of Nigeria.

In the Southwestern part, the associated kingdoms of Oyo and Benin were also well established by the fifteenth century, developing from common origins in Ife, the sacred capital of the Yoruba people. A bit obscure is the early history of the Igbo people in the Southeastern part of the forest belt, whose purely village society was based on a system of communal land holding. Somehow, a complex social and political pattern had developed among the peoples of what is now Nigeria by the time the earliest European expeditions reached the coast in search of gold.

Slaves were initially West Africa's principal export commodity, and the trade was to continue for over 300 years with British ships handling most of the traffic by the early eighteenth century. A consequence of the slave-trade was the creation of Delta States, a number of large trading ports which became dependent on the European slave-traders for their economic survival.

In the hinterland, civil war ravaged the Yoruba States, culminating in the disintegrating of the Oyo Empire.

In the North a Jihad (Muslim Holy War) was launched under the leadership of the Fulani. Meanwhile, European influences were gaining foothold in the South as the volume of legitimate trade increased.

In 1861 the British annexed Lagos, declaring, it a colony. Later, the Nigerian area was declared a British 'Sphere of Influence' covering various regions of this area.

The political entity known as Nigeria came into existence in 1914 with the amalgamation of the Northern and Southern British Protectorates. With the amalgamation of the separate administration of Northern and Southern Protectorate on 1 January 1914, the Colony and Protectorate of Nigeria came under a unitary administration presided over by Lord Lugard as Governor General. The main aims of the amalgamation were to extend to the South the Native Authority System established by Lugard as High Commissioner in the North from 1900 to 1906 and to provide technical services on an all Nigeria basis. Lieutenant - Governors were appointed for Southern and Northern Nigeria and these two parts remained largely separate units. However, a wholly advisory 'Nigerian Council' was created to cover all Nigeria and its thirty six members included six unofficial European and six unofficial African members. This arrangement was not considered a success, and in 1922 it was replaced by a Legislative Council for the Colony and Southern part of the protectorate.

The Legislative Council included Ten unofficial African members (out of a total of Forty-six) of whom three were elected by Lagos and one by Calabar on a franchise limited to males with a gross income of at least $ 100 (N200) a year, a British subject or native of the Protectorate. Lagos and Calabar were singled out for the grant of the franchise because these towns had relatively higher concentrations of educated elites who demanded and got representation in their country's legislatures.

The Legislative powers of the new Council were restricted to the Colony and Southern Nigeria (the Governor legislating directly for the North), but much of its legislation (e.g., relating to customs duties) effected the North. Its official members included the Lieutenant Governor and certain senior officials from the North, but had no African unofficial members from that part of Nigeria, even after amalgamation. Northern Nigeria thus remained a substantially separate administration within the new Nigeria.

The constitutional arrangement initiated in 1922 remained substantially unchanged until 1946; but toward the end of World War II increasingly, vigorous criticism of these arrangements came from African organisations outside the Legislative Council. The reform effected in 1946 was, however, essentially the work of then Governor, Sir Arthur Richards (as he was then known) whose avowed purpose was:-

To promote the unity of Nigeria, to provide adequately within that unity for the diverse elements which make up the country and to secure greater participation by Africans in the discussion of their own affairs.

A Legislative Council whose competence and membership covered the whole of Nigeria was established, twenty-eight of its members were to be unofficial, four of whom would continue to be directly elected by Lagos and Calabar (though on a reduced franchise of $50 (N100), twenty were to be selected by the regional council in each of the three Regions which has resulted in 1939 from the division of Southern Nigeria into Eastern and Western Provinces. Richards argued that a central legislature was not enough.

Nigeria falls naturally into three regions, the North, the West and the East, and the people of those regions differ widely in tribe, in custom, in outlook, and in their traditional system of government.

In addition to the bicameral Regional Council in the North, he accordingly established single chamber councils in the East and West called the House of Assembly.

In all Regional Houses of Assembly, there were unofficial (and African) majorities, but they consisted of members selected by the Native Authorities. The Regional Councils had no legislative powers but only limited financial ones. Executive power remained in the hands of British officials at the centre as well as in the Regions.

The Modern Development Of Politics

Although its roots can be traced much farther back, the modern development of politics in Nigeria dates essentially from the later part of Word War II and the reactions of the enactment of the Richard's Constitution. The earliest political organisations grew up in Lagos where the Nigeria National Democratic Party (NNDP) was formed under the leadership of Herbart Macauley to contest the 1922 Elections. This was followed in 1937 by the Nigerian Youth Movement (NYM), a largely Yoruba organisation which succeeded an earlier Lagos Youth Movement, under the leadership of H.O. Davies, which successfully contested the Lagos Municipal Elections of 1938 against the Nigeria National Democratic Party. A legislative Council bye Election in 1941 produced dissensions within the NYM and in the Lagos Town Council elections of 1943, the Democratic Party resumed control. In 1944 under the impetus of Nigerians who returned from abroad an attempt was made to create national front and the National Council of Nigeria and Cameroun's (NCNC) was founded in August 1944 under the leadership of Herbert Macauley and Nnamdi Azikiwe. Its aim was to set up a broad-based political movement to promote Nigerian self government within the British Commonwealth.

The NCNC attacked the new constitution because of the constitution's failure to enlarge the electorate and extend the principle of direct elections, apart from its other defects. An undertaking had been given that the constitution would be reviewed after nine years but in 1948 the new Governor, Sir John Macpherson, agreed that changes be introduced in three years. One of the principal complaints against the Richard's Constitution was that it was not the outcome of consultation with the leaders of Nigerian opinion. Special arrangements for ascertaining the views of all sections of the population were, therefore, accordingly proposed and these took place throughout 1949 and much of 1950.

The new Constitution enacted in 1951 established Legislatures in each of the three Regions which were empowered to legislate on specified subjects (such as agriculture, social services, local government, etc). Members of the Central Legislature were elected from their own members by the Regional Legislature (sixty-eight from North and thirty-four by each of the two Southern Regions). The proportion of nominated and unofficial members both in the Central and Regional Legislatives was reduced. In each Region and at the Centre there were African Ministers who formed the majority of the appropriate executive councils; but the governors continued to preside. At the Centre each Region was represented by an equal number of three Ministers and one for Southern Cameroun.

Thus in 1959, the Federation consisted of three big Regions, namely the Northern (the biggest), Eastern and Western Regions, with Lagos serving as the Federal Capital Territory. As stated earlier on, this tripartite administrative structure began to emerge in 1951 with the introduction of the Macpherson Constitution of that year. With subsequent amendments made at various constitutional conferences held in London and Nigeria, the 1954 Federal Constitution emerged, under which the first nationwide federal election of that year was held under the auspices of the various regional governments which naturally ensured the perpetuation of their control of their respective regions. The Northern Peoples Congress (NPC) won in the North, the Action Croup (AG) in the West and the National Council of Nigeria and Cameroun's (NCNC) won in the Eastern Region.

These political parties emerged not too long before the elections and, in fact, the introduction of the Macpherson's Constitution with its promise of transfer of real political power to Nigerians, acted as a catalyst for the growth of new political parties in Nigeria. The Action Group made its debut on the political scene in March 1951 having metamorphosed into a political party from a Yoruba cultural organisation known as Egbe Omo Oduduwa which was founded by Chief Awolowo in London in 1945. Chief Awolowo became the first President of both the Egbe and the AG which also drew support from members of the Nigerian Youth Movement, one of the then political parties in the country whose main activities were centred in Lagos and its environs.

The Northern Peoples Congress has its origin in the Jam'iyyar Mutanen Arewa (Congress of the Northern Peoples) which had been formed in 1949 by some educated Northerners, notably Abubakar Tafawa Balewa, Yahaya Gusau and Dr. R.A.B Dikko. The congress was intended to be a cultural organisation and not a political one, but was declared a political party in October 1951 on the eve of the indirect election which was about to take place throughout the country to select members of the newly created Houses of Assembly (Regional Legislatures) from amongst whom members of the Central Legislature were to be selected.

The three major parties could not possibly be sufficient to cater for all the diverse ethnic and cultural groups which made up Nigeria. The years following 1951 saw the emergence of many local parties representing one minority interest or the other and most of them had little influence outside their town or district. However, in 1959 thirteen minority parties managed to contest the federal election for that year. They were the Northern Elements Progressive Union (NEPU), United Middle Belt Congress (UMBC), Bornu Youth Movement (BYM), all in the Northern Region, also the Mobolaje Grand Alliance and Otu Edo in the West and the United National Independence Party and the Democratic Party of Nigeria and Cameroun's in the East.

Triumphs And Turmoil

Both the 1959 and 1979 Federal Elections had special significance for Nigeria in that each marked an important watershed in the political and social development of the country. The 1959 election preceded the grant of political independence to the country in 1960, after the expiration of the '99 year lease' or the enforced occupation of Nigeria by the British, which began with the annexation of Lagos in 1861 and culminated in the surrender of the Sultan of Sokoto forces on 15 March 1903. The 1979 Federal Election, on the other hand, was a prelude to the return of the control of government to the democratically elected representatives of the people, after more than thirteen years of military rule. The terrain between the two watersheds was pockmarked with several craters that will forever remain as prominent features of the Nigerian political land mass. These features included a turbulent general election in

1964, three successful military coups in January 1966, July 1966 and July 1975, and an abortive one in February 1976, during which many prominent civilians and military personnel were assassinated, or executed by firing squads. There was the civil war between July 1967 and January 1970 which cost over a million lives. There was also the conduct of two controversial national population censuses in 1963 and 1973; the result of the first one was accepted by the Federal (civilian) Government and two of the then three Regional Governments (North and West) but rejected by the East. The results of the 1973 census was accepted by the Federal Military Government headed by General Yakubu Gowon but later rejected by the leaders of the military coup who toppled Gowon from power on 29 July 1975.

On the positive side, during the period 1959-79, Nigeria experienced tremendous economic growth witnessed by unprecedented expansion of infrastructural facilities such as roads, airports, electricity generating capacity, as well as expansion of educational facilities at primary, secondary and tertiary levels. The growth of the industrial and commercial sectors of the economy was phenomenal, encouraged by the industrial and commercial policies pursued by the various governments, including the progressive 'indigenisation' of foreign business enterprises. The growth of the Gross National Product which provided funds for capital investment in the various sectors of the economy was made possible by the increase in the production of petroleum in the country, which began in about 1956 and whose production reached about 550,000 barrels per day before the civil was and over 2 million barrels per day in 1979.

Independence

The first of the great events that occurred between 1959 and 1979 (apart from the two federal elections of those years) was the granting of political independence to Nigeria on 1 October 1960. It was the culmination of Nigerian perseverance and British statesmanship that ushered the birth of the Nigerian nation without bloodshed or extreme bitterness as was the case elsewhere in colonial Africa.

The achievement of independence, some say, 'on a platter of gold' was Nigeria's first triumph, soon to be followed by a succession of turmoil's including going to the edge or brink of the cliff but not tumbling over on a number of occasions; such as the post - 1964 election crisis, the 1963/64 census controversy and, of course, the coups d' etat of January 1966 and July 1966. These also included the civil disturbances as well as the civil war 1967 - 70, and an abortive coup of 1976. The triumph showed in managing to keep the country one and intact while also successfully, immediately after a long period of civil war, embarking on the execution of gigantic economic, social and political programmes which vastly expanded the infrastructural facilities in the country.

Nigeria was granted independence by the British colonialists on 1st October, 1960. The leaders of independence struggle became the founding fathers of the Federation of Nigeria. They include Dr Nnamdi Azikiwe, Abubakar Tafawa Balewa, Ahmadu Bello Sardauna of Sokoto, Obafemi Awolowo, Dr Michael Okpara, Ladoke Akintola, Aminu Kano, J.S Tarka, Anthony Enahoro, Aliyu Makaman Bida, amongst others.

At independence in 1960 the Federation of Nigeria comprised three Regions namely, Northern Region, Western Region, Eastern Region: This tripartite structure was later increased to:-

(a) 4 in 1963 with the creation of the Mid Western Region;

(b) 12 in 1967 by the Military Administration of General Yakubu Gowon on the eve of the outbreak of the civil war;

(e) 19 in 1976 by the Military Administration of General Murtala Mohammed;

(d) 21 in 1987 by the Military Administration General Ibrahim Babangida;

(e) 30 in 1991 by the Military Administration of General Ibrahim Babangida;

(f) 36 in 1996 by the Military Administration of General Sani Abacha. The Federal Capital was moved from Lagos to Abuja after creation of Abuja Federal Capital Territory (FCT) in 1976.

Thus Nigeria now consists of 36 Federating Units and FCT, Abuja.

The Federating Units, together with their respective Local Government Areas/Area Councils and State Capitals are listed in the First Schedule, parts 1 and 2 of the 1999 Constitution of the Federal Republic of Nigeria. The Schedule forms Annex A to this memorandum.

The Land Area or Landmass of Nigeria is 923,768 sq. Km (356,669 sq. Miles). The coastline is 853 Km (530 miles whilst the highest point at Dimlang is 2042 M/6699 ft., on Mambila Plateau. Other prominent geographical features include the following principal rivers - Niger, Benue, Kaduna, Sokoto - Rima, Gongola, Ogun, Osun, Cross River, Hadeja, Jemaare, Imo, Anambra, Gurara. At the north eastern corner of the country lays Lake Chad.

The largest state in terms of landmass is Niger State which covers 76,363 sq. Km. Lagos State is the smallest which covers 3,345 sq. Km. Abuja Federal Capital Territory is 7,315 sq. Km. The Land areas of all the 36 States and Abuja FCT, together with other details pertaining to them is given in Table 3.4 .The Population according to the 2006 National Census is 140,431,790 comprising of 71,345.488 males and 69,086,302 females. The 2006 Census Final Results is published in the Supplement of Federal Republic of Nigeria Official Gazette No. 2, Vol. 96 dated 2nd February, 2009. It forms Table 3.3 to this book.

The first Independence Constitution of Nigeria, 1960 was based on the British Westminster model, with a ceremonial Governor - General, representing the Queen of England who was technically Nigerian Head of State, and an Executive Prime Minister who was Head of the Government of the Federation. Dr. Nnamdi Azikiwe. Azikiwe was Governor-General whilst Alh. Abubakar Tafawa Balewa became Prime Minister. At regional levels there were ceremonial governors for the Northern, Western, Eastern Regions and Regional Premiers as Heads of Regional Governments. The Independence Constitution was replaced by the Republican Constitution when Nigeria became a Federal Republic in 1963. The Governor-General became President and Ceremonial Head of State of Nigeria, no longer owing any allegiance to the Queen of England. The Republican Constitution was also based on the British Westminster model.

The Westminster model provides for the election of Head of Federal Government or Prime Minister from a federal constituency and Head of Regional Government from a regional constituency, as a member of the Federal House of Representatives or Regional House of Assembly, respectively. Elected members of each political party select their parliamentary leader who becomes Head of Government, if his political party commands a majority of members in the House. Further, all ministers/parliamentary secretaries (junior ministers) are members of parliament but under the Presidential system, Ministers/Commissioners are appointed by President/Governor from outside the House.

The military intervened in January 1966 and removed the civilians from governance of the country. The military abolished the constitution and ruled by Decrees, in effect turning the country into a quasi-unitary state, though nominally a federal republic appointing military governors to govern at state levels but who received instructions from the Federal Military Government which called the shots.

Before handing over to the civilians the Military constituted a constituent Assembly of partly elected/selected representatives which, under the guidance of the military produced the 1979 Constitution of the Federal Republic of Nigeria. This constitution was based on the American Presidential system with a powerful executive president at the centre and equally powerful governors at the state levels. This arrangement was replicated at the local government levels with powerful local government chairmen. Nigeria has been operating the executive presidential model from 1979 to date but was modified to quasi-unitary system during the long period of military rule from 1983 to 1999 when the current 1999 Constitution of the Federal Republic of Nigeria was promulgated by decree.

The 1999 Constitution provides for Three Arms of Government with separation of powers as one of its cardinal principles. The Arms are:-

(a) The Executive headed by a powerful President who appoints Ministers, Special Advisors, Assistants, Permanent Secretaries and other aides to assist him in governing the country;

(b) The Judiciary- headed by the Chief Justice of Nigeria, with Justices of the Supreme Courts, Court of Appeal and Federal High Court, who constitute the Judicial Arm of government;

(c) The Legislature which is bicameral, comprising the Senate and House of Representatives, together forming the National Assembly.

The Senate or Upper Chamber consists of 109 Senators, three elected from each of the 36 States of the Federation and one from the Federal Capital, Abuja. The House of Representatives comprises 360 members elected from the states and Abuja, the number representing each federating unit, depending on the population of the unit. The membership ranges from 24 each for Kano and Lagos states, being the most populous to as low as 8 or less for smaller states. Abuja FCT has six members representing its Area Councils.

The Economy

Currently the Nigerian economy is mainly based on production of one commodity - oil. That was not the case from the 1950's to early 1970's when agriculture held sway. The then regions established agricultural produce Marketing Boards to purchase and sell various agricultural products such as groundnuts, cotton, benni-seed, soya beans, ginger in the North, cocoa, palm kernels, palm oil and other palm produce in the West and East.

In a decade 1960 - 70 marked by outstanding political, constitutional and economic changes, one strikingly constant factor is the economic dominance of the marketing boards, not only in the regions, but in the international trade of the country. The commodities handled by all the regional marketing boards, accounted for about two - thirds of Nigeria's

total exports and have contributed significantly to the total resources available for development projects. However, with the discovery of oil in the country in 1958 and its exploitation since then, agriculture was relegated to the background with regards to the foreign exchange earnings, though it still contributes quite a lot to the Gross Domestic Product (GDP) of Nigeria. However, during the last few years, especially since 2007 more attention is being paid by the federal and state authorities to the development of agriculture and this effort seems to be paying dividends. According to Economist Diary 2009, Nigeria ranks:-

(a) 2nd in the production of sorghum (2006), producing 9,866,000 metric tones (MT.) out of 56,485,000 MT. total World production.

(b) 4th in the production of cocoa, producing 485,000 MT. out of 4,059,000 MT. World production.

(c) 2nd in the production of millets, producing 7,705,000 MT. out of 31,781,000 MT. World production.

(d) 2nd in the production of sweet potatoes producing 3.462,000 MT. out of 123,510,000 MT. World production.

(e) 1st in the production of cassava, producing 45,721,000 MT. out of 226,337,000 MT. World production.

(f) 4th in the production of groundnuts producing 1,520,000 MT. out of 33,870,000 MT. World production.

If the current efforts by federal and state governments on the development of agriculture are sustained and enhanced, Nigeria can regain her rightful position amongst the nations of the world in the production of primary products for domestic consumption and exports. Indeed agriculture may surpass oil as the country's main foreign exchange earner for the country.

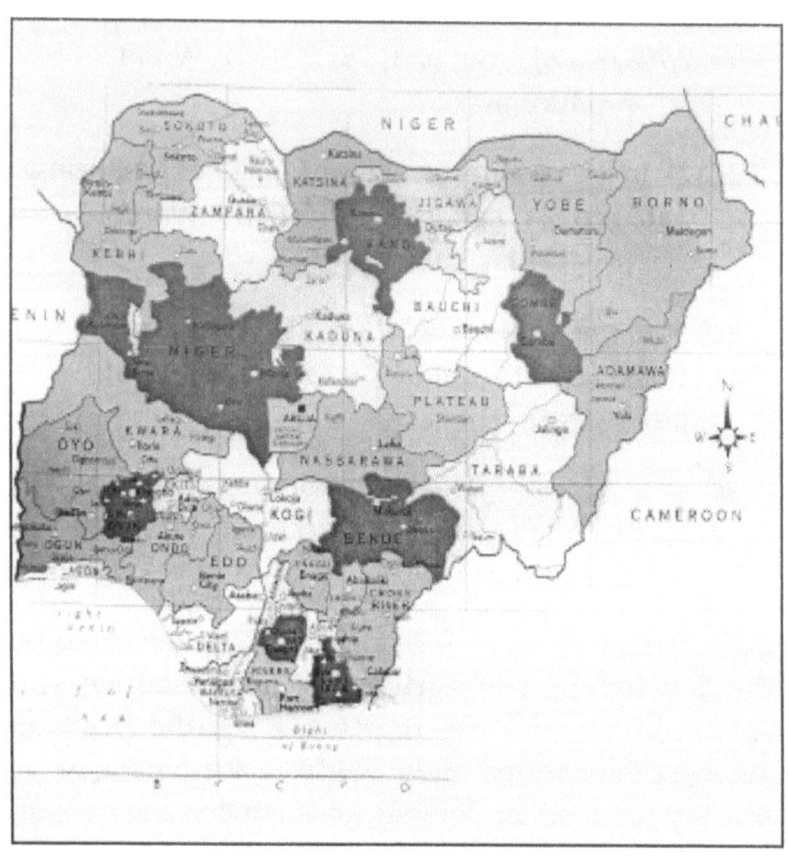

Figure 3.1: Map of Nigeria showing the 36 states and Abuja

Education

Nigerian governments have since the 1950's embarked on the development and expansion of the education sector at primary, secondary and tertiary levels. The number of schools, colleges, universities as well as enrolment of pupils/students has witnessed phenomenal growth.

Nigeria has numerous federal - or state funded universities. The oldest, university of Ibadan, was founded in 1948 as a college of the University of London and became autonomous in 1962. Many of the other prominent universities - University of Nigeria in Nsukka, Obafemi Awolowo University (formerly university of lfe), Ahmadu Bello University in Zaria, and University of Lagos were founded in the years immediately following independence in 1960. In 1970 the University of Benin was opened, followed in 1975 by new universities in Calabar, Ilorin, Jos, Kano, Maiduguri, Port Harcourt and Sokoto. Since 1980, several more universities have opened, including institutes specialising in agriculture and technology. A variety of polytechnic schools, including Yaba College of Technology in Lagos and Kaduna Polytechnic, offer non-degree post secondary school programmes.

Source - Microsoft Corporation 1993- 2008.

Nigeria can now boast of 104 recognised universities - owned by federal and state governments as well as private sector. However the quality of products of educational institutions of higher learning does not seem to match the quantity. Every effort should be made by governments and the private sector to marry the two.

Elections

Nigeria had held elections at local, regional, state and federal levels in 1951. 1954, 1959, 1964, 1979, 1983, 1991/1993, 1997, 1999, 2003 and 2007. Some of these elections were conducted under the supervision of departing colonial power, military regimes 1959, 1979, 1991/3, 1997/99 whilst others 1964, 1983, 2003, 2007,2011 were held by incumbent civilian governments. However, as pointed out by President Umaru Musa Yar' Adua, during the inauguration of the Electoral Reform Committee (headed by Hon. Justice M.I. Uwais, former Chief Justice of Nigeria) on 28th August, 2007: "One sad recurrent feature of our political developmental history has been the consistence with which every general election result has been disputed and contested. Beginning with 1959 general elections, almost every poll has suffered controversy resulting from real and perceived flaws, structural and institutional inadequacies and sometimes deficiencies in the electoral laws and even the constitution'.

The Electoral Reform Committee was mandated by the President to "examine the entire electoral process with a view to ensuring that we raise the quality and standard of our general elections and thereby deepen our democracy".

The Committee submitted its report to the President in December 2008 and averred that it "is firmly convinced that the acceptance and implementation of the recommendations contained in this Report will significantly restore credibility in the electoral process and usher in an era of free, fair and credible elections in the country".

It had been reported in the media that the federal Government had accepted and/or noted 73 of the 83 major recommendations and forwarded a number of electoral reform bills to the National Assembly for enactment into laws after due deliberation in the usual manner.

Mining

Petroleum dominates the Nigerian economy: Virtually 100 percent of export earnings and about four - fifths of government revenues are derived from petroleum. Fluctuations in world oil prices therefore have a dramatic effect on the Nigerian economy. Discovered in 1956, petroleum was produced at a rate of 818 million barrels in 2004 from more than 150 oil fields, mostly in the Niger Delta. About one fifth of the oil fields are offshore. Although Nigeria's petroleum is expensive to produce, it commands a high price because of its low sulphur content. Half of all exports go to the United States, and most of the other half to Europe.

Nigeria has Africa's largest reserves of natural gas, most of which are associated with the oil fields. Despite efforts to develop markets for natural gas - including investment in gas - fired electrical installations, a liquefied natural gas (LNG) plant, and fertilizer and chemical ventures — about three-quarters of gas production is burned off rather than diverted for use.

Production of coal has declined to about 64,000 metric tons, far less than the late 1950's production, largely because the Enugu coalfields are almost exhausted. The government is attempting to boost production by developing new fields at Lafia and Obi in Benue State (now

Nasarawa state). Also in sharp decline are production of tin (3,000 metric tons per year) and columbite, which have been mined from alluvial gravels on the Jos Plateau since 1905 but which now yield about one percent of their late - 1960's levels. Other major mining operations include iron ore, which is exploited for the steel industry, and limestone, used to manufacture cement. Gypsum, barite, and kaolin are also mined.

Manufacturing

In 2003, manufacturing accounted for 4 percent of the GDP, down from 13 percent in 1982. Pre-independence Nigeria, its large population notwithstanding, had very little industrial development; a few tanneries and oil-crushing mills that processed raw materials for export. During the 1950s and 1960s a few factories, including the first textile mills and food-processing plants, opened to serve Nigerians. During the 1970s and early 1980s industrial production increased rapidly, principally in Lagos, Kaduna, Kano, and Port Harcourt. Factories also appeared in smaller, peripheral cities such as Calabar, Bauchi, Katsina, Akure, and Jebba, due largely to government policies encouraging decentralisation (although these policies sometimes ran counter to solid economic criteria).

Nigeria's major manufactures are food and beverages, cigarettes, textiles and clothing, soaps and detergents, footwear, wood products, motor vehicles, chemical products, and metals. Smaller - scale manufacturing businesses engage in weaving, leather making, pottery making, and woodcarving. The smaller industries are often organised in craft guilds involving particular families, who pass skills from generation to generation.

In an attempt to broaden Nigeria's industrial base, the government has invested heavily in joint ventures with private companies since the early 1980s. The largest such project is the integrated steel complex at Ajaokuta, built in 1983 at a cost of $4 billion. The government has also invested heavily in petroleum refining, petrochemicals, fertilizers, and implements for assembling automobiles and farm equipment. Government policies have hampered industrial development by making it difficult to obtain sufficient raw materials and spare parts. Partly as a result, only a fraction of the country's manufacturing capacity is currently utilized, In the mid 1990's the government introduced a series of reforms, including an allowance tor greater foreign ownership in Nigerian industries, a loosening of controls on foreign exchange, and the establishment of an export—processing zone at Calabar.

Energy

Petroleum, natural gas and hydroelectricity are Nigeria's major sources of commercial energy, they are slightly outpaced by the largely non-commercial consumption of fuel wood and charcoal. Despite major programs to extend electricity demand outstrips supply, in part because of mismanagement in the government agency overseeing energy production. In the late 1990s periodic power outages cost Nigerian factories countless hours of operation. The major thermal electrical installations are at Egbin. Afam, and Sapele. Hydroelectricity is generated at Kainji Dam and in lesser quantities at Shiroro Gorge on the Kaduna River, at Jebba, and at several smaller sites. Only a small percentage of the country's potential hydroelectric capacity has been developed.

Transportation

Nigeria has 193,200km (120,049M) of roads. Most Nigerians travel by bus or taxi both between and within cities. During the 1970s and 1980s federal and state governments built and upgraded numerous expressways and trans-regional trunk roads. State governments also upgraded smaller roads, which helped open rural areas to development. However, by the mid — 1990s lack of investment had left most of the roads to deteriorate. Nigeria has 3,528km (2,192mi) of operated railway track. The main line, completed in 1911, links Lagos to Kano, with extensions from Kano to Nguru, from Zaria to Kauran Namoda, and from Minna to Baro. The use of railways, both for passenger and freight traffic, has declined due to competition from the road network. Nigeria's largest ocean ports are at Lagos (Apapa and Tin Can Island), Port Harcourt, Calabar Sapele, and Warri. The main petroleum- exporting facilities are at Bonny and Burutu. Transportation along inland waterways, especially in Niger and Benue rivers, was very important during the colonial era. In the late 1980s the government upgraded river ports at Onitsha, Ajaokuta, Lokoja, Baro, Jebba and Yelwa. Locks have been constructed at Kainji Dam to facilitate navigation. River transport is used mainly for shipping goods. Nigeria has four international airports: in the Lagos suburb of Ikeja, in Abuja, in Port-Harcourt and in Kano. Internal flights serve the majority of state capitals, of which Kaduna, and Enugu are the busiest. Private airlines offer both domestic and international flights.

Communication

The first newspaper was founded in Lagos in the 1830s. Today, Nigerians choose from dozens of daily and weekly newspapers published across the country, most in English, but several in Nigerian languages, especially Hausa and Yoruba. The Daily Times, published in Lagos, was the newspaper with the largest circulation. Despite sporadic government censorship and partial government ownership of some newspapers, the press has remained relatively free and has often been outspoken in its criticism of the government.
(Note - Daily Times has ceased publication).

The national government began broadcasting in 1957, when it established a chain of radio stations. Most of the country's numerous radio and television stations continue to be operated by the government. Programs are available in English, Hausa, Yoruba, Igbo and several other Nigerian languages. The country's international radio service, Voice of Nigeria, also broadcasts in several languages.

In 2005 there were only 9.3 telephone mainlines for every 1,000 people in Nigeria. About one-third of the telephones were in Lagos. Major cities in all parts of the country are linked by a system of domestic satellites, microwave towers, and coaxial cables; however, the telephone system is unreliable because of poor service and maintenance at the local level. (Note - Since 2002 mobile telephones operated by private companies have raised the number of telephones lines to over 82 million).

Currency And Banking

The national currency of Nigeria is the naira which is divided into 100 kobo (154 naira equal U.S $1; 2011 average). Exchange rates have been allowed to fluctuate. Attempt to fix the rate at 22 naira per dollar failed. Currency and banking are supervised by the Central Bank of Nigeria, founded in 1958 and located in Lagos, (now in Abuja). Several foreign banks have branches in Nigeria, since 1976, all have been required to have at least 60 percent Nigerian ownership. The Nigerian Stock Exchange, founded in 1960, is located in Lagos and is supervised by the Nigerian Securities and Exchange Commission.

Source: (D) to (K) 2008 Microsoft Corporation.

Administration

From 1960 to date, Nigeria has had the following civilian and military administrations at the federal level and many such administrations at state levels.

1st Civilian Administration:- headed by Alhaji Abubakar Tafawa Balewa with Dr. Nnamdi Azikiwe as ceremonial Governor - General and later President 1960- 1966.

1st Military Administration:- headed by Major General Aguiyi - Ironsi -Jan 1966-July 1966.

2nd Military Administration:- headed by Lt. Col. Yakubu Gowon (later General) July 1966- July 1975.

3rd Military Administration:- headed by Brigadier (later General) Murtala Mohammed-July 1975 - Feb. 1976.

4th Military Administration:- headed by General

Olusegun Obasanjo —February 1976 - October 1979.

2ⁿᵈ Civilian Administration:- headed by Alhaji Shehu Shagari October 1979 - December 1983.

5th Military Administration:- headed by Major General Muhammadu Buhari Dec. 1983 - August 1985.

6ᵗʰ Military Administration:- headed by General Ibrahim Babangida August 1985 - August 1993.

Interim Civilian Administration:- headed by Chief Ernest Shonekan Aug. 1993 - Nov. 1993.

7ᵗʰ Military Administration:- headed by General Sani Abacha Nov. 1993 -June 1998.

8th Military Administration:- headed by General Abdussalmi Abubakar June 1998 -May 1999.

3rd Civilian Administration:- headed by Chief Olusegun Obasanjo May 1999 - May 2007.

4th Civilian Administration:- headed by Alhaji Umaru Musa Yar' Adua May 2007 to May 2010 and from May 2007 headed by Goodluck Ebele Jonathan.

Table 3.1: Local Government Areas in Nigeria

SCHEDULES

State	Local Government Areas	Capital City
Abia	Aba North, Aba South, Arochukwu, Bende, Ikwuano, Isiala-Ngwa North, Isiala-Ngwa South Isuikwuato, Obi Ngwa, Ohafia, Osisioma Ngwa Ugwunagbo, Ukwa East, Ukwa West, Umuahia North, Umuahia South, Umu-Nneochi	Umuahia
Adamawa	Demsa, Fufore, Ganye, Girei, Gombi, Guyuk, Hong, Jada, Lamurde, Madagali, Maiha, Mayo Belwa, Michika, Mubi North, Mubi South, Numan Shelleng, Song, Toungo, Yola North, Yola South	Yola
Akwa Ibom	Abak, Eastern Obolo, Eket, Esit Eket, Essien Udim, Etim Ekpo, Etinan, Ibeno, Ibesikpo Asutan, Ibiono Ibom, Ika, Ikono, Ikot Abasi, Ikot Ekpene, Ini, Itu, Mbo, Mkpat Enin, Nsit Atai, Nsit Ibom, Nsit Ubium, Obot Akara, Okobo, Onna, Oron, Oruk Anam, Udung Uko, Ukanafun, Uruan, Urue –Offong/Oruko, Uyo.	Uyo
Anambra	Aguata, Anambra East, Anambra West, Anaocha, Awka North, Awka South, Ayamelum, Dunukofia, Ekwusigo, Idemili North, Idemili South Ihiala, Njikoka, Nnewi North, Nnewi South, Ogbaru, Onitsha South, Ogbaru, Onitsha North, Onitsha South, Orumba North, Orumba South, Oyi.	Awka
Bauchi	Alkaleri, Bauchi, Bogoro, Damban, Darozo, Dass, Gamawa, Ganjuwa, Giade, Itas/Gadau, Jama'are, Katagum, Kirfi, Misau, Ningi, Shira Tafawa-Balewa, Toro, Warji, Zaki	Bauchi
Bayelsa	Brass, Ekeremor, Kolokuma/Opokuma, Nembe, Ogbia, Sagbama, Southern Ijaw, Yenegoa	Yenegoa

State	Local Government Areas	Capital
Benue	Ado, Agatu, Apa, Buruku, Gboko, Guma, Gwer East, Gwer West, Katsina-Ala, Konshisha, Kwande, Logo, Makurdi, Obi, Ogbadibo, Oju, Okpokwu, Ohimini, Oturkpo, Tarka, Ukum, Ushongo, Vandeikya	Makurdi
Borno	Abadam, Askira/uba, Bama, Bayo, Biu Chibok Damboa, Dikwa, Gubio, Guzamala, Gwoza, Hawul, Jere, Kaga, Kala/Balge, Konduga, Kukawa, Kwaya Kusar, Mafa, Magumeri, Maiduguri, Marte, Mobbar, Monguno, Ngala, Nganzai, Shani	Maiduguri
Cross River	Abu Akamkpa Alpabuyo Bakassi, Bekwara, Base Bokk Calabar Municipal, Calabar South Etung, Ikom Obanliku, Obubra, Obudu Odukpani, Ogoja, Yakuu, Yala.	Calabar
Delta	Aniocha North Aniocha South, Bomadi, Burutu Ethiope East, Ethiope West, Ika North East, Ika South, Isoko North, Isoko South, Ndokwa East Ndokwa West, Okpe, Oshimili North Oshimili South, Patani, Sapele, Udu, Ughelli North Ughelli South, ukwuani, Uvwie, Warri North Warri South, Warri South West.	Asaba
Ebonyi	Abakaliki Afikpo North, Afikpo South, Ebonyi Ezza North, Ezza South, Ikwo, Ehieh Ivo, Izzi Ohaozara, Ohaukwu, Onicha.	Abakaliki
Edo	Akoko-Edo, Egor, Esan Central, Esan North East, Esan South East, Esan West Etsako Central, Etsako East, Etsako West, Igueben, Ikpoba-Okha Oredo, orhiommwon, Ovia, North East, Ovia South West, Owan East Owan West Uhunmwonde	Benin City
Ekiti	Ado Ekiti, Aiyekire Efon, Ekiti East Ekiti South West, Ekiti West Emure, Ido-Osi, Ijero, Ikere Ikole, Ikejemeji, Irepodun/Ifelodun Ise/Orun, Moba, Oye	Ado Ekiti

State	LGAs	Capital
Enugu	Aniru Awgu, Enugu East Enugu North, Enugu South, Ezeagu, Igbo-Ekiti, Igbo-Eze North Igbo-Eze South, Isi-Uzo, Nkanu East, Nkanu West, Nsukka, Oji-River, Udenu, Udi, Uzo-Uwani	Enugu
Gombe	Akko, Balanga, Billiri, Dukku, Funakaye, Gombe Kaltungo, Kwami, Nafada, Shomgom, Yamaltu/Deba	Gombe
Imo	Aboh-Mbaise Ahiazu Mbaise, Ehime-Mbano, Exinihitte, Ideato North, Ideato South Ihitte/Uboma, Ikeduru, Isiala Mbano, isu, Mbaitoli, Ngor-Okpala, Njaba Nwangele, Nkwerre, Obowo, Oguta, Obani/Igbama, Okigwe Orlu, Orsu Out East, Oru West, Owerri Municipal, Owerri North, Owerri West, Unuimo	Owerri
Jigawa	Auyo, Babura, Birnin Kuda, Birinwa Buji, Gagarawa, Garki gunnel, Guri, Gwaram, Gwiwa, Hadejia, Lahun Kafin Hausa Kaugama, Kazame Kayawa, Magatari, Malam Madon Miga Rmgam, Ron Sule-Tankarkar, Bama Yankwashi.	Dutse,
Kaduna	Bimin Gwari, Chikun, Giwa, Igabi, Ikara, Jaba Jema'a, Kachia, Kaduna North, Kaduna South Kagarko, Kajuru, Kaura, Kauru, Kubau, Kudan, Lere, Makarfi, Sabon-Gari, Sanga, Soba, Zangon-Kataf, Zaria	Kaduna
Kano	Ajingi, Albasu, Bagwai, Bebeji, Bichi, Bunkure, Dala, Dambatta, Dawakin Kudu, Dawakin Tofa Doguwa, Fagge, Gabasawa, Garko, Garum Mallam, Gaya, Gezawa, Gwale, Gwarzo, Kabo, Kano Municipal, Karaye, Kibiya, Kiru, Kumbotso, Kunchi, Kura, Madobi, Makoda, Minjibir, Nasawara, Rano, Rimin Gado, Rogo, Shanono, Sumaila, Takai, Tarauni, Tofa, Tsanyawa, Tudun Wada, Ungogo, Warawa, Wudil	Kano
Katsina	Bakori, Batagarawa, Batsari, Baure, Bindawa Charachi, Dandume, Danja, Dan Musa, Daura	Katsina

	Dutsi, Dutsin-Ma, Faskari, Funtua, Ingawa, Jibia, Kafur, Kaita, Kankara, Kankia, Katsina, Kurfi, Kusada, Mai'Adua, Malumfashi, Mani, Mashi, Matazu, Musawa, Rimi, Sabuwa, Safana, Sandamu Zango	
Kebbi	Aleiro, Arewa-Dandi, Argungu, Augie, Bagudo Birnin Kebbi, Bunza, Dandi, Fakai, Gwandu, Jega Kalgo, Koko/Besse, Maiyama, Ngaski, Sakaba, Shanga, Suru, Wasagu/Danko, Yauri, Zuru.	Birnin Kebbi
Kogi	Adayi Ajaokuta, Ankpa Bassa, Dekina, Ibaji Idah, Igalamela-Odolu, Ijumu, Kabba/Bunu, Kogi Lokoja, Mopa-Muro, Ofu, Ogori/Magongo, Okehi, Okene, Olamabolo, Omala, Yagba East, Yagba West	Lokoja
Kwara	Asa, Baruten, Edu, Ekiti, Ifelodun, Ilorin East Ilorin South, Ilorin West, Irepodun, Isin, Kaiama, Moro, Offa, Oke-Ero, Oyun, Pategi	Ilorin
Lagos	Agege, Ajeromi-Ifelodun, Alimosho, Amuwo Odofin, Apapa, Badagry, Epe, Eti-Osa, Ibeju/Lekki, Ifako –Ijaye, Ikeja, Ikorodu, Kosofe, Lagos Island Lagos Mainland, Mushin, Ojo, Oshodi-Isolo. Shomolu, Surelere.	Ikeja
Nasarawa	Akwanga, Awe, Doma, Karu, Keana, Keffi Kokona, Lafia, Nasarawa, Nasarawa-Eggon, Obi, Toto, Wamba.	Lafia
Niger	Agaie, Agwara, Bida, Borgu, Bosso, Chanchaga, Edati, Gbako, Gurara, Katcha, Kontagora Lapai, Lavun, Magama, Mariga, Mashegu, Mokwa, Muya, Paikoro, Rafi, Rijau, Shiroro, Suleja, Tafa, Wushishi.	Minna
Ogun	Abeokuta North, Abeokuta South, Ado-Odo/Ota, Egbado North, Egbado South, Ewekoro, Ifo, Ijebu East, Ijebu North, Ijebu North East, Ijebu Ode, Ikenne, Imeko-Afon, Ipokia, Obafemi-Owode, Ogun Waterside, Odeda, Odogbolu, Remo North Shagamu.	Abeokuta

Ondo	Akoko North East, Akoko North West, Akoko South East, Akoko South West, Akure North, Akure South, Ese-Odo, Idanre, Ifedore, Ilaje, Ile-Oluji-Okeigbo, Irele, Odigbo, Okitipupa, Ondo East, Ondo West, Ose, Owo	Akure
Osun	Aiyedade, Aiyedire, Atakumosa East, Atakumosa-West, Boluwaduro, Boripe, Ede North, Ede South, Egbedore, Ejigbo, Ife Central, Ife East, Ife North Ife South, Ifedayo, Ifelodun, Ila, Ilesha East, Ilesha West, Irepodun, Irewole, Isokan, Iwo, Obokun, Odo-Otin, Ola-Oluwa, Olorunda, Oriade, Orolu, Osogbo.	Osogbo.
Oyo	Afijio, Akinyele, Atiba, Atigbo, Egbeda, Ibadan Central, Ibadan North, Ibadan North West, Ibadan South East, Ibadan South West, Ibarapa Central Ibarapa East, Ibarapa North, Ido, Irepo, Iseyin, Itesiwaju, Iwajowa, Kajola, Lagelu, Ogbomoso North, Ogbomoso South, Ogo Oluwa, Olorunsogo, Oluyole, Ona-Ara, Orelope, Ori Ire, Oyo East, Oyo West, Saki East, Saki West Surulere.	Ibadan
Plateau	Barikin Ladi, Bassa, Bokkos, Jos East, Jos North Jos South, Kanam, Kanke, Langtang North, Langtang South, Mangu, Migang, Pankshin, Qua'an Pan, Riyom, Shendam, Wase.	Jos
Rivers	Abua/Odual, Ahoada East, Ahoada West, Akuku Toru, Andoni, Asari-Toru, Bonny, Degema Emohua, Eleme, Etche, Gokana, Ikwerre Khana Obia/Akpor, Ogba/Egbema/Ndoni, Ogu/Bolo, Okrika, Omumma, Opobo/Nkoro, Oyigbo, Port-Harcourt Tai.	Port-Harcourt
Sokoto	Binji, Bodinga, Dange-shuni, Gada, Goronyo Gudu, Gwadabawa, Illela, Isa, Kware, Kebbe, Rabah, Sabon Birni, Shagari, Silame, Sokoto North. Sokoto South, Tambuwal, Tangaza, Tureta, Wamakko, Wurno, Yabo.	Sokoto

Taraba	Ardo-Kola, Bali, Donga, Gashaka, Gassol, ibi, Jalingo, Karim-Lamido, Kurmi, Lau, Sardauna, Takum, Ussa, Wukari, Yorro, Zing.	Jalingo
Yobe	Bade, Bursari, Damaturu, Fika, Fune, Geidam Gujba, Gulani, Jasusko, Karasuwa, Machina, Nangere, Nguru, Potiskum, Tarmua, Yunusari, Yusufari.	Damaturu
Zamfara	Anka, Bakura, Birnin Magaji, Bukkuym, Bungudu, Gummi, Gusau, Kaura Namoda, Maradun, Maru, Shinkafi, Talata Mafara, Tsafe, Zunmi	Gusau

PART II
DEFINITION OF FEDERAL
CAPITAL TERRITORY, ABUJA

The definition of the boundaries of the Federal Capital Territory, Abuja referred to under Chapters 1 and VIII of this constitution is as follows-
Starting from the village called izom on 70'e lontitude and 9' 15 latitude project a straight line westward to a point just north of lehu on kemi river, then project a line a line along 6' 471/2'e southward passing close to the villages called semasu, zui and bassa down to a place a little west of Abaji town; thence project a line along parallel 8°27½'N Latitude to Ahinza village 7° 30'N Latitude and 7° 20'E Longitude; thence draw a line northwards joining the villages of Odu, Karshi and Karu. From Karu the line shall proceed along the boundary between the Niger and Plateau states as far as Kawu; thence the line shall proceed along the boundary between Kaduna and Niger states up to point just north of Bwari village; thence the line goes straight to Zuba village and thence straight to Izom.

2. **FEDERAL CAPITAL TERRITORY, ABUJA**

Area Councils

Area Council	Headquarters
Abaji	Abaji
Abuja Municipal	Garki
Bwari	Bwari
Gwagwalada	Gwagwalada
Kuje	Kuje
Kwali	Kwali

FEDERAL REPUBLIC OF NIGERIA
OFFICIAL GAZETTE

No. 2 Abuja – 2nd February, 2009 Vol. 96

Government Notice No. 2

This is published as Supplement to uns Gazette

S.I.	No Short Title	Page
1.	Legal Notice on Publication of 2006 Census Final Results	B1-42

Printed and Published by The Federal Government Printer, Abuja, Nigeria FGP 16/22009/10,000 (OL02)

Annual Subscription from 1st January, 2009 is Local: N15,000.00 Overseas, N21,500.00 (Surface Mail) N24,500.00 (Second Class Air Mail). Present issue N2,000 per copy. Subscribers who wish to obtain Gazette after 1st January should apply to the Federal Government Printer, Abuja for amended Subscriptions.

Table 3.2: Result of 2006 Population Census

Population By State And Sex

S/No	State	Both Sexes	Male	Female
1	ABIA	2,845,380	1,430,298	1,415,082
2	ADAMAWA	3,178.950	1,607,270	1,571,680
3	AKWA IBOM	3.902,051	1,983,202	1,918,849
4	ANAMBRA	4,177,828	2,117,984	2,059,844
5	BAUCHI	4,653,066	2,369,266	2,283,800
6	BAYELSA	1,704,515	874,083	830,432
7	BENUE	4,253,641	2,144,043	2,109,598
8	BORNO	4,171,104	2,163,358	2,007.746
9	CROSS RIVER	2,892,988	1,471,967	1,421,02'
10	DELTA	4,112,445	2,069,309	2,043,136
11	EBONYI	2,176,947	1,064,156	1,112,791
12	EDO	3,233,366	1,633,946	1,599,420
13	EKITI	2,398.957	1,215,487	1,183,470
14	ENUGU	3,267,837	1,596,042	1,671,795
15	GOMBE	2,365,040	1,244,228	1,120,812
16	IMO	3,927,563	1,976,471	1,951,092
17	JIGAWA	4,361,002	2,198,076	2,162,926
18	KADUNA	6,113,503	3,090,438	3,023.065
19	KANO	9,401,288	4,947,952	4,453,336
20	KATSINA	5,801,584	2,948,279	2,853,305
21	KEBBI	3,256,541	1,631,629	1,624,912
22	KOGI	3,314,043	1,672,903	1,641,140
23	KWARA	2,365,353	1,193,783	1,171,570
24	LAGOS	9,113,603	4,719,125	4,394,480
25	NASRAWA	1,869,377	943,801	925,576
26	NIGER	3,954,772	2,004,350	1,950,422
27	OGUN	3,751,140	1,864,907	1,886,233
28	ONDO	3,460,877	1,745,057	1,715,820
29	OSUN	3,416,959	1,734,149	1,682,810
30	OYO	5,580,894	2,802,432	2,778,462
31	PLATEAU	3,206,531	1,598,998	1,607,533
32	RIVERS	5,198,716	2,673,026	2,525,690
33	SOKOTO	3,702,676	1,863,713	1,838,963
34	TARABA	2,294,800	1,171,931	1,122,869
35	YOBE	2,321,339	1,205,034	1,116,305
36	ZAMFARA	3,278,873	1,641,623	1,637,250
37	FCT ABUJA	1,406,239	733,172	673,067
	NIGERIA	**140,431,790**	**71,345,488**	**69,086,302**

Table 3.3: Population By Local Government Area and Sex

ABIA

LGA	Both Sexes	Male	Female
Aba North	106,844	53,016	53,828
Aba South	427,421	220,541	208,880
Arochukwu	169,339	85,695	83,644
Bende	192,621	95,675	96,946
Ikwuano	137,897	70,509	67,388
Isiala-Ngwa North	154,083	76,261	77,822
Isiala-Ngawa South	136,650	67,205	69,445
Isiukwuato	115,794	56,660	59,134
Obi Ngwa	181,894	89,593	92,301
Ohafia	245,987	124,416	121,571
Osisioma Ngwa	220,662	110,790	109,872
Ugwunagbo	85,371	42,801	42,570
Ukwa East	58,139	29,410	28,729
Ukwa West	87,367	44,149	43,218
Umuahia North	223,134	112,595	110,539
Umuahia South	139,058	68,950	70,108
Umu-Nneochi	163,119	82,032	81,087
Abia State	**2,845,380**	**1,430,298**	**1,415,082**

ADAMAWA

LGA	Both Sexes	Male	Female
Demsa	178,407	89,511	88,896
Fufore	209,460	105,626	103,834
Ganye	169,948	85,798	84,150
Girei	129,855	66,906	62,949
Gombi	147,787	74,399	73,388
Guyuk	176,505	89,440	87,065
Hong	169,183	83,736	85,447
Jada	168,445	82,882	85,563
Lamurde	111,254	56,495	54,759
Madagali	135,142	67,134	68,008
Maiha	110,175	55,622	54,553
Mayo-belwa	152,803	75,399	77,404
Michika	155,238	75,036	80,202

Mubi North	151,515	78,059	73,456
Mubi South	129,956	66,553	63,403
Numan	91,549	47,512	44,037
Shelleng	148,490	75,143	73,347
Song	195,188	97,228	97,960
Toungo	52,179	26,598	25,581
Yola Noth	199,674	108,379	91,295
Yola South	196,197	99,814	96,383
Adamawa State			**1,571,680**

AKWA IBOM

LGA	Both Sexes	Male	Female
Abak	139,069	70,305	68,764
Eastern Obolo	59,970	30,229	29,741
Eket	172,856	89,006	83,850
Esit-Eket	63,358	32,189	31,169
Essien Udim	198,257	97,888	95,369
Etim Ekpo	105,922	53,514	52,408
Etinan	168,924	85,760	83,164
Ibeno	74,840	40,006	34,834
Ibesikpo Asutan	137,127	69,681	67,446
Ibiono Ibom	188,605	96,106	92,499
Ika	72,772	36,996	35,776
Ikono	131,673	66,080	65,593
Ikot Abasi	132,608	67,806	64,802
Ikot Ekpene	141,408	71,738	69,670
Ini	99,084	50,108	48,976
Itu	127,856	65,410	62,446
Mbo	102,173	52,351	49,822
Mkpat Enin	177,293	89,283	88,010
Nsit Atai	73,395	37,186	36,209
Nsit Ibom	108,095	55,197	52,898
Nsit Ubium	127,083	64,674	62,409
Obot Akara	147,286	74,392	72,894
Okobo	102,753	52,395	50,358
Onna	123,193	61,413	61,780
Oron	87,209	44,545	42,664
Oruk Anam	171,839	86,863	84,976
Udung Uko	53,060	27,613	25,447
Ukanafun	125,473	63,308	62,165

ANAMBRA

LGA	Both Sexes	Male	Female
Aguata	369,972	187,262	182,710
Anambra East	152,149	77,539	74,610
Anambra West	167,303	85,833	81,470
Anaocha	284,215	142,961	141,254
Awka North	112,192	57,219	54,973
Awka South	189,654	95,902	92,752
Ayamelum	158,152	81,065	77,087
Dunukofia	96,517	40,476	47,041
Ekwusigo	158,429	80,053	78,376
Idemili North	431,005	219,223	211,782
Idemili South	206,816	105,830	100,986
Ihiala	302,277	152,200	150,077
Njikoka	148,394	73,869	74,525
Nnewi North	155,443	77,517	77,926
Newi South	233,362	118,532	114,830
Ogbaru	223,317	115,678	107,639
Onitsha North	125,918	61,588	64,330
Onitsha South	137,191	71,348	65,843
Orumba North	172,773	81,996	87,777
Orumba South	184,548	93,199	91,349
Oyi	168,201	83,694	82,507
Anambra State	4,177,828	1,117,984	2,059,844

BAUCHI

LGA	Both Sexes	Male	Female
Alkaleri	328,284	165,936	161,348
Bauchi	493,730	252,420	241,310
Bogoro	83,809	41,776	42,033
Damban	150,212	75,978	74,234
Darazo	249,946	125,741	123,205
Dass	90,114	45,695	43,419
Gamawa	284,411	145,510	138,901
Ganjuwa	278,471	140,402	138,069
Giade	156,022	70,628	76,394
Itas Gadau	228,527	114,808	113,719
Jama'nre	117,482	60,941	56,541
Katagum	293,920	152,552	140,468
Kirfi	145,636	75,337	70,299

Misau	261,410	135,704	125,706
Ningi	385,997	196,528	189,469
Shira	233,999	118,888	115,111
Tafawa Balewa	221,310	119,372	110,938
Toungo			
Yola North			
Yola South			
Adamawa State	**3,178,950**	**1,607,270**	**1,571,680**

BAUCHI

LGA	Both Sexes	Male	Female
Alkaleri	328,284	165,936	161,348
Bauchi	493,730	252,420	241,310
Bogoro	83,809	41,776	42,033
Damban	150,212	75,978	74,234
Darazo	249,946	126,741	123,205
Dass	90,114	45,695	43,419
Gamawa	284,411	145,510	138,901
Ganjuwa	278,471	140,402	138,069
Giade	156,022	79,628	76,394
Itas Gadau	228,527	114,808	113,719
Jama'are	117,482	60,941	56,541
Katagum	293,920	152,552	140,468
Kirfi	145,636	75,337	70,299
Misau	261,410	135,704	125,706
Ningi	385,997	196,528	189,469
Shira	233,999	118,888	115,111
Tafawa-Balewa	221,310	119,372	110,938
Toro	346,000	172,921	173,079
Warji	714,983	58,054	56,929
Zaki	189,703	97,075	92,628
Bauchi State	**4,653,066**	**2,369,266**	**2,283,800**

BAYELSA

LGA	Both Sexes	Male	Female
Brass	184,127	94,359	89,768
Ekeremor	269,588	137,753	131,835
Kolokuma/Opokuma	79,266	39,925	39,314
Nembe	130,966	66,768	64,198
Ogbia	179,606	92,015	87,591

LGA	Both Sexes	Male	Female
Sagama	186,869	95,667	91,202
Southern Ijaw	321,808	165,329	156,479
Yenegoa	352,285	182,240	170,045
Bayelsa State	**1,704,515**	**874,083**	**830,432**

BENUE

LGA	Both Sexes	Male	Female
Ado	184,389	92,367	92,022
Agatu	115,597	58,478	57,119
Apa	96,780	48,658	48,122
Buruku	206,215	103,655	102,560
Gboko	361,325	180,669	180,656
Guma	194,164	97,318	96,846
Gwer East	168,660	85,287	83,373
Gwer West	122,313	61,764	60,549
Katsina-Ala	225,471	114,093	111,378
Konshisha	226,492	114,192	112,300
Kwande	248,642	125,442	123,200
Logo	169,570	86,069	83,501
Makurdi	300,377	154,138	146,239
Obi	98,707	49,143	49,564
Ogbadibo	130,988	64,847	66,141
Ohimini	70,688	35,876	34,812
Oju	168,491	84,220	84,271
Okpokwu	175,596	89,193	86,403
Oturkpo	266,411	136,612	129,799
Tarka	79,280	39,783	39,497
Ukum	216,983	108,728	108,255
Ushongo	191,935	96,062	95,873
Vandeikya	234,567	117,449	117,118
Benue State	**4,253,641**	**2,144,0423**	**2,109,598**

BORNO

LGA	Both Sexes	Male	Female
Abadam	100,065	53,749	46,316
Askira/Uba	143,313	72,676	70,637
Bama	270,119	136,524	133,595
Bayo	79,078	39,287	39,791
Biu	175,760	90,609	85,151
Chibok	66,333	33,952	32,381
Damboa	233,200	125,873	107,321
Dikwa	105,042	55,160	49,882

Gubio	151,286	78,893	72,393
Guzamala	95,991	50,254	45,737
Gwoza	276,568	143,407	133,161
Hawul	120,733	59,611	61,122
Jeer	209,107	107,714	101,393
Kaga	89,996	47,150	42,846
Kala/Balge	60,834	31,260	29,574
Konduga	157,322	80,017	77,305
Kukawa	203,343	109,287	94,056
Kwaya Kusar	56,704	29,007	27,697
Mafa	103,600	53,351	50,249
Magumeri	140,257	72,510	67,749
Maiduguri	540,016	282,409	257,607
Marte	129,409	67,777	61,632
Mobbar	116,633	61,426	55,207
Monguno	109,834	57,146	52,688
Ngala	236,498	122,127	114,371
Nganzai	99,074	50,822	48,252
Shani	100,989	51,360	49,629
Borno State	**4,171,104**	**2,163,358**	**2,007,746**

CROSS RIVER

LGA	Both Sexes	Male	Female
Abi	144,317	73,077	71,240
Akamkpa	149,705	76,921	72,784
Akpabuyo	272,262	141,602	130,660
Bakassi	31,641	18,175	13,466
Bekwara	105,497	52,914	52,583
Biase	168,113	85,625	82,488
Boki	186,611	95,154	91,457
Calabar–Municipal	183,681	93,092	90,589
Calabar South	191,515	94,584	96,931
Etung	80,036	41,089	38,947
Ikom	163,691	82,646	81,045
Obanliku	109,633	55,998	53,635
Obubra	172,543	87,153	85,390
Obudu	161,457	81,537	79,920
Odukpani	192,884	100,697	92,187
Ogoja	171,574	86,802	84,772
Yakuri	196,271	99,485	96,786

Yala	211,557	105,416	106,141
Cross River State	**2,892,988**	**1,471,967**	**1,421,021**

DELTA

LGA	Both Sexes	Male	Female
Aniocha North	104,062	52,448	51,614
Aniocha South	142,045	69,224	72,821
Bomadi	86,016	43,435	42,581
Burutu	207,977	106,169	101,808
Ethiope East	200,942	101,596	99,346
Ethiope West	202,712	102,750	99,962
Ika North East	182,819	91,431	91,388
Ika South	167,060	82,214	84,846
Isoko North	143,559	71,948	71,611
Isoko South	235,147	119,167	115,980
Ndokwa East	103,224	52,306	50,918
Ndokwa West	150,024	73,842	76,182
Okpe	128,398	65,270	63,128
Oshimili North	118,540	58,101	60,439
Oshimili South	150,032	76,078	73,954
Patani	67,391	34,307	33,084
Sapele	174,273	86,167	88,106
Udu	142,480	71,813	70,667
Ughelli North	320,687	160,550	160,137
Ughelli South	212.638	107,730	104,908
Ukwuani	119,034	58,890	60,144
Uvwie	188,728	93,999	94,729
Warri North	136,149	70,446	65,703
Warri South	311,970	158,402	153,568
Warri South West	116,538	61,026	55,512
Delta State	**4,122,445**	**2,069,309**	**2,043,136**

EBONYI

LGA	Both Sexes	Male	Female
Abakaliki	149,683	72,518	77,165
Afikpo North	156,649	80,632	76,017
Afikpo South	157,542	79,093	78,449
Ebonyi	127,226	60,388	66,838
Ezza North	146,149	70,341	75,808
Ezza South	133,625	66,373	67,252
Ikwo	214,969	99,855	115,114

Ishielu	152,581	72,671	79,910
Ivo	121,363	62,049	59,314
Izzi	236,679	112,832	123,847
Ohaozara	148,317	75,093	73,224
Ohaukwu	195,555	94,479	101,076
Onicha	236,609	117,832	118,777
Ebonyi State	**2,176, 947**	**1,064,156**	**1,112,791**

EDO

LGA	Both Sexes	Male	Female
Akoko-Edo	261,567	132,184	129,383
Egor	340,287	168,925	171,362
Esan Central	105,242	53,017	52,225
Esan North East	121,989	61,647	60,342
Eason South East	166,309	84,587	81,722
Esan West	127,718	65,312	62,406
Etsako Central	94,228	47,708	46,520
Etsako East	147,335	72,477	74,858
Etsako West	198,975	100,986	97,989
Igueben	70,276	35,132	35,144
Ikpoba-okha	372,080	184,725	187,355
Oredo	374,515	188,895	185,620
Orhionmwon	183,994	92,433	91,561
Ovia North East	155,344	80,433	74,911
Ovia South West	138,072	72,113	65,959
Owan East	154,630	78,890	75,740
Owan West	99,056	50,755	48,301
Uhunmwonde	121,749	121,749	58,022
Edo State	**3,233,366**	**1,633,366**	**1,599,420**

EKITI

LGA	Both Sexes	Male	Female
Ado Ekiti	313,690	162,563	151,127
Aiyekire (Gbonyin)	147,999	75,342	72,657
Efon	87,187	43,587	43,600
Ekiti East	138,340	70,022	68,318
Ekiti South West	165,087	83,416	81,671
Ekiti West	179,600	91,241	88,359
Emure	94,264	47,767	46,497
Ido-Osi	160,001	81,461	

Ijero	221,873	112,363	
Ikere	148,558	69,252	
Ikole	170,414	86,873	
Ilejemeji	43,459	22,010	
Irepodun/Ifelodun	131,330	66,289	
Ise/Orun	113,951	57,743	
Moba	145,408	75,747	
Oye	337,796	69,661	
Ekiti State	**2,398,957**	**1,215,487**	**1,183,470**

ENUGU

LGA	Both Sexes	Male	Female
Aniniri	136,221	66,225	69,996
Awgu	197,292	96,132	101,160
Enugu East	277,119	131,214	145,905
Enugu North	242,140	118,895	123,245
Enugu South	198,032	93,758	104,274
Ezeagu	170,603	84,466	86,137
Igbo-Ekiti	208,333	105,262	103,071
Igbo-Eze North	258,829	126,069	132,760
Igbo-Eze South	147,364	72,619	74,745
Isi-Uzo	148,597	72,497	76,100
Nkanu East	153,591	75,008	78,583
Nkanu West	147,385	72,706	74,679
Nsukka	309,448	149,418	160,030
Oji-River	128,741	61,719	67,022
Udenu	178,687	88,381	90,306
Udi	238,305	117,914	120,391
Uzo-Uwani	127,150	63,759	63,391
Enugu State	**3,267,837**	**1,596,042**	**1,671,795**

GOMBE

LGA	Both Sexes	Male	Female
Akko	337,435	177,515	159,920
Balanga	211,490	108,494	102,996
Billiri	202,680	103,201	99,479
Dukku	207,658	107,583	100,075
Funakaye	237,687	132,054	105,633
Gombe	266,844	146,721	120,123
Kaltungo	160,392	80,177	80,215
Kwami	193,995	99,778	94,217

GOMBE continued

LGA	Both Sexes	Male	Female
Nafada (Bajoga)	140,185	79,009	61,176
Shomgom	150,948	76,450	74,498
Yamaltu/Deba	255,726	133,246	122,480
Gombe State	**2,365,040**	**1,244,228**	**1,120,812**

IMO

LGA	Both Sexes	Male	Female
Aboh-Mbaise	194,779	98,480	96,299
Ahiazu-Mbaise	170,824	86,326	84,498
Ehime-Mbano	130,575	65,237	65,338
Ezinihitte	168,767	84,725	84,042
Ideato North	156,161	78,753	77,408
Ideato South	159,654	81,125	78,529
Ihitte/Uboma	119,419	60,492	58,927
Ikeduru	149,737	75,025	74,712
Isiala Mbano	197,921	100,835	97,086
Isu	164,328	84,299	80,029
Mbaitoli	237,474	118,959	118,515
Ngor-Okpala	157,858	78,829	79,029
Njaba	143,485	72,401	71,084
Nkwerre	80,270	40,845	39,425
Nwangele	127,691	65,022	62,669
Obowo	117,432	58,204	59,228
Oguta	142,340	72,549	69,791
Ohaji/Egbema	182,891	92,604	90,287
Okigwe	132,701	67,660	65,041
Orlu	142,792	69,632	73,160
Orsu	120,224	60,490	59,734
Oru East	111,743	56,148	55,595
Oru West	115,704	59,108	56,596
Owerri North	176,334	87,094	89,240
Owerri West	101,754	49,968	51,786
Owerri-Municipal	125,337	60,882	64,455
Unuimo	99,368	50,779	48,589
Imo State	**3,927,563**	**1,976,471**	**1,951,092**

JIGAWA

LGA	Both Sexes	Male	Female
Auyo	132,268	67,409	64,859
Babura	212,955	106,373	106,582
Birniwa	142,015	73,864	68,151
Birnin Kudu	314,108	153,997	160,111
Buji	97,284	48,984	48,300
Dutse	251,135	125,773	125,362
Gagarawa	82,153	41,529	40,624
Garki	150,261	74,734	75,531
Gwaram	271,368	135,785	133,583
Gwiwa	128,730	64,760	63,970
Hadejia	104,286	54,171	50,115
Jahun	229,882	113,694	116,188
Kafin Hausa	267,284	135,012	132,272
Kaugama	128,981	64,592	64,389
Kazaure	161,161	82,513	78,648
Kiri Kasamma	192,583	98,430	94,153
Kiyawa	172,952	87,862	85,090
Maigatari	177,057	89,722	87,335
Malam Madori	164,791	85,165	79,626
Miga	127,876	63,067	64,809
Ringim	192,407	95,581	96,826
Roni	77,414	39,618	37,796
Sule-Tankarkar	134,813	65,985	68,828
Taura	131,861	66,107	65,754
Yankwashi	95,643	48,062	47,581
Jigawa State	**4,361,002**	**2,198,076**	**2,162,926**

KADUNA

LGA	Both Sexes	Male	Female
Birnin-Gwari	258,581	130,919	127,662
Chikun	372,272	187,433	184,839
Giwa	292,384	145,608	146,776
Igabi	430,753	217,414	213,339
Ikara	194,723	95,598	99,125
Jaba	155,973	77,415	78,558
Jema'a	278,202	140,724	137,478
Kaehia	252,568	127,624	124,944
Kaduna North	364,575	187,075	177,500
Kaduna South	402,731	204,969	197,762

LGA	Both Sexes	Male	Female
Kagarko	239,058	121,041	118,017
Kajuru	109,810	54,506	55,304
Kaura	174,626	88,565	86,061
Kauru	221.276	111,119	110,157
Kubau	280,704	141,528	139,176
Kudan	138,956	71,704	67,252
Lere	339,740	170,396	169,344
Makarfi	146,574	73,292	73,282
Sabon-Gari	291,358	149,111	142,247
Sanga	151,485	76,482	75,003
Soba	291,173	145,145	146,028
Zangon-Kataf	318,991	161,870	157,121
Zaria	406,990	210,900	196,090
Kaduna State	**6,113,503**	**3,090,438**	**3,023,065**

KANO

LGA	Both Sexes	Male	Female
Ajingi	172,610	86,605	86,005
Albasu	187,639	94,862	92,777
Bagwai	161,533	83,511	78,022
Babeji	191,916	97,351	94,565
Bichi	278,309	139,346	138,963
Bunkure	174,467	87,185	87,282
Dala	418,759	237,943	180,816
Dambatta	210,474	105,538	104,936
Dawakin Kudu	225,497	116,109	109,388
Dawakin Tofa	246,197	126,390	119,807
Doguwa	150,645	77,849	72,796
Fagge	200,095	111,859	88,236
Gabasawa	211,204	107,869	103,335
Garko	161,966	82,025	79,941
Garun Mallam	118,622	71,515	47,107
Gaya	207,419	105,199	102,220
Gezawa	282,328	143,380	138,948
Gwale	357,827	219,201	138,626
Gwarzo	183,624	94,669	88,955
Kabo	153,158	83,156	70,002
Kano Municipal	371,243	219,636	151,607
Karaye	144,045	71,727	72,318
Kibiya	138,618	70,942	67,676
Kiru	267,168	140,565	126,603

LGA	Both Sexes	Male	Female
Kamboso	294,391	166,171	128,220
Kunchi	110,170	55,221	54,949
Kura	143,094	76,921	66,173
Madobi	137,685	71,095	66,590
Mokoda	220,094	110,014	110,080
Minjibir	219,611	108,218	111,393
Nasarawa	596,411	323,740	272,671
Rano	148,276	75,997	72,279
Rimin Gado	103,371	53,245	50,126
Rogo	227,607	113,104	114,503
Shanono	139,128	68,466	70,662
Sumaila	250,379	125,162	125,217
Takai	202,639	100,269	102,370
Tarauni	221,844	122,069	99,775
Tofa	98,603	49,870	48,733
Tsanyawa	157,730	80,638	77,092
Tuden Wada	228,658	113,791	114,867
Ungogo	365,737	192,372	173,365
Warawa	131,858	66,800	65,058
Wudil	188,639	100,357	88,282
Kano State	**9,401,288**	**4,947,952**	**4,453,336**

KATSINA

LGA	Both Sexes	Male	Female
Bakori	149,516	72,714	76,802
Batagarawa	189,059	96,693	92,366
Batsari	207,874	104,279	103,595
Baure	202,941	102,127	100,814
Bindawa	151,002	76,925	74,077
Charanchi	136,989	70,040	66,949
Dan Musa	113,190	58,031	55,159
Dandume	145,323	74,222	71,101
Danja	125,481	63,663	61,818
Daura	224,884	115,576	109,308
Dutsi	120,902	61,430	59,472
Dustin-Ma	169,829	88,202	81,627
Faskari	194,400	97,963	96,437
Funtua	225,156	117,789	107,367
Ingawa	169,148	86,061	83,087
Jibia	167,435	85,149	82,286

Kafur	209,360	104,620	104,740
Kaita	182,405	93,190	89,215
Kankara	243,259	121,815	121,444
Kankia	151,395	77,061	74,334
Katsina	318,132	168,906	149,226
Kurfi	116,700	59,021	57,679
Kusada	98,348	50,930	47,418
Mai'adua	201,800	103,107	98,693
Malumfashi	182,891	92,420	90,471
Mani	176,301	88,007	88,294
Mashi	171,070	84,105	86,965
Matazu	113,814	57,587	56,227
Musawa	170,006	85,788	84,218
Rimi	154,092	77,059	77,033
Sabuwa	140,679	72,106	68,573
Safana	185,207	93,410	91,797
Sandamu	136,944	68,512	68,432
Zango	156,052	79,771	76,281
Katsina State	**5,801,584**	**2,948,279**	**2,853,305**

KEBBI

LGA	Both Sexes	Male	Female
Aleiro	67,078	34,368	32,710
Arewa-Dandi	189,728	94,825	94,903
Argungu	200,248	99,658	100,590
Augie	116,368	58,185	58,183
Bagudo	238,014	118,733	119,281
Birnin Kebbi	268,620	135,426	133,194
Bunza	123,547	61,309	62,238
Dandi	146,211	72,907	73,304
Fakai	119,772	60,441	59,331
Gwandu	151,077	74,610	76,467
Jega	197,757	96,936	93,821
Kalgo	84,928	42,262	42,666
Koko/Besse	158,818	78,419	76,3999
Maiyama	173,759	85,728	88,031
Ngaski	126,102	62,480	63,622
Sakaba	91,728	46,194	45,534
Shanga	127,142	63,478	63,664
Suru	148,474	72,912	75,562

Wasagu/Danko	265,271	131,388	133,883
Yauri	100,564	53,016	47,548
Zuru	165,335	86,354	78,981
Kebbi State	**3,256,541**	**1,631,629**	**1,624,912**

KOGI

LGA	Both Sexes	Male	Female
Adayi	217,219	108,891	168,328
Ajaokuta	122,432	62,995	59,437
Ankpa	266,176	133,705	132,471
Bassa	139,687	70,293	69,394
Dekina	260,968	131,394	129,574
Ibaji	127,572	64,423	63,149
Idah	79,755	40,141	39,614
Igalamela-Odolu	147,048	74,489	72,559
Ijumu	118,593	59,582	59,011
Kabba/Bunu	144,579	72,639	71,940
Kogi	115,100	58,864	56,236
Lokoja	196,643	101,145	95,498
Mopa-Mura	43,760	22,311	21,449
Ofu	191,480	96,671	94,809
Ogori/Magongo	39,807	20,051	19,756
Okehi	223,574	112,879	110,695
Okene	325,623	163,935	161,688
Olamabolo	158,490	78,439	80,051
Omala	107,968	54,366	53,602
Yagba East	147,641	74,619	73,022
Yagba West	139,928	71,071	68,857
Kogi State	**3,314,043**	**1,672,903**	**1,641,140**

KWARA

LGA	Both sexes	Male	Female
Asa	124,668	62,751	61,917
Baruten	206,679	104,727	101,952
Edu	201,642	104,040	97,602
Ekiti	54,399	27,611	26,788
Ifelodun	204,975	103,650	101,325
Ilorin East	207,462	104,801	102,661

Ilorin South	209,251	103,606	105,645
IlorinWest	365,221	180,387	184,834
Lrepodun	147,594	73,554	74,040
Lsin	59,481	30,088	29,393
Kaiama	124,015	64,901	59,114
Moro	108,715	54,860	53,855
Offa	88,975	44,813	44,162
Oke-ero	56,970	28,358	28,612
Oyun	94,454	47,890	46,564
Pategi	110,852	57,746	53,106
Kwara State	**2,365,353**	**1,193,783**	**1,171,570**

LAGOS

LGA	Both sexes	Male	Female
Agege	461,743	238,456	223,287
Ajeromi-Ifelodun	687,316	352,273	335,043
Alimosho	1,319,571	665,750	653,821
Amuwo-Odofin	328,975	173,742	155,233
Apapa	22,986	123,163	99,823
Badagry	237,731	119,821	117,910
Epe	181,734	91,925	89,809
Eti-Osa	283,791	158,858	124,933
Ibeju/Lekki	117,793	60,729	57,064
Ifako-Ijaye	427,737	219,109	208,628
Ikeja	317,614	171,782	145,832
Ikorodu	527,917	268,463	259,454
Kosofe	682,772	358,935	323,837
Lagos Island	212,700	110,042	102,658
Lagos Mainland	326,700	170,568	156,132
Mushin	631,857	326,873	304,984
Ojo	609,173	315,401	293,772
Oshodi-Isolo	629,061	325,207	303,854
Shomolu	403,569	207,519	196,050
Surulere	502,865	260,509	242,356
Lagos State	**9.113,605**	**4,719,125**	**4,394,480**

NASARAWA

LGA	Both sexes	Male	Female
Akwanga	111,902	56,135	55,767
Awe	113,083	57,326	55,757
Doma	138,991	71,395	67,596
Karu	216,230	109,515	106,715
Keana	81,801	40,873	40,928
Keffi	92,550	47,527	45,023
Kokona	108,558	54,379	54,179
Lafia	329,922	165,631	164,291
Nasarawa	187,220	95,105	92,115
Nasarawa-Eggon	148,405	74,543	73,862
Obi	148,977	74,675	74,302
Toto	119,051	59,884	59,167
Wamba	72,687	36,813	35,874
Nasarawa State	**1,869,377**	**943,801**	**925,576**

NIGER

LGA	Both Sexes	Male	Female
Agaie	132,098	66,703	65,395
Agwara	57,347	29,293	28,054
Bida	185,553	93,741	91,812
Borgu	172,835	87,327	85,508
Bosso	148,136	75,033	73,103
Chanchaga	202,151	105,265	96,886
Edati	159,818	80,615	79,203
Gbako	126,845	63,871	62,974
Gurara	90,879	45,153	45,726
Katcha	120,893	60,526	60,367
Kontagora	151,968	77,782	74,186
Lapai	117,021	59,974	57,047
Lavun	209,777	107,146	102,631
Magama	181,470	90,740	90,730
Mariga	199,600	100,899	98,701
Mashegu	215,197	107,909	107,288
Mokwa	242,858	123,467	119,391
Muya	103,461	52,584	50,877
Paikoro	158,178	79,399	78,779
Rafi	186,118	94,395	91,723
Rijau	176,199	88,875	87,324
Shiroro	235,665	118,640	117,025

LGA	Both Sexes	Male	Female
Suleja	215,075	112,030	103,045
Tafa	83,874	41,524	42,350
Wushishi	81,756	41,459	40,297
Niger State	**3,954,772**	**2,004,350**	**1,950,422**

OGUN

LGA	Both Sexes	Male	Female
Abeokuta North	198,793	96,463	102,330
Abeokuta South	250,295	119,977	130,318
Ado-Odo/Ota	527,242	261,523	265,719
Egbado North	183,844	89,880	93,964
Egbado South	168,336	81,666	86,670
Ewekoro	55,093	28,212	26,881
Ifo	539,170	269,206	269,964
Ijebu East	109,321	56,981	52,340
Ijebu North	280,520	141,074	139,446
Ijebu North East	68,800	34,581	34,219
Ijebu Ode	157,161	76,466	80,695
Ikenne	119,117	60,607	58,510
Imeko-Afon	82,952	41,850	41,102
Ipokia	150,387	74,649	75,738
Obafemi-Owode	235,071	118,574	116,497
Odeda	109,522	55,200	54,322
Odogbolu	125,657	63,838	61,819
Ogun Waterside	74,222	37,412	36,810
Remo North	59,752	29,893	29,859
Shagamu	255,885	126,855	129,030
Ogun State	**3,751,140**	**1,864,907**	**1,886,233**

ONDO

LGA	Both Sexes	Male	Female
Akoko North East	179,092	92,456	86,636
Akoko North West	211,867	107,076	104,791
Akoko South East	82,443	42,175	40,268
Aoko South West	228,383	114,733	113,650
Akure North	130,765	66,526	64,239
Akure South	360,268	178,672	181,596
Ese-Odo	158,256	79,812	78,444
Idanre	129,795	67,531	62,264
Ifedore	176,372	89,574	86,798
Ilaje	289,838	145,859	142,979

Ile-Oluji-Okeigbo	171,876	87,104	84,772
Irele	144,136	72,861	71,275
Odigbo	232,287	116,299	115,988
Okitupupa	234,138	117,594	116,544
Ondo East	76,092	38,851	37,241
Ondo West	288,878	141,759	147,109
Ose	144,139	73,119	71,020
Owo	222,262	112,056	110,206
Ondo State	**3,460,877**	**1,745,057**	**1,715,820**

OSUN

LGA	Both Sexes	Male	Female
Aiyedade	149,569	76,032	73,537
Aiyedire	76,309	38,299	38,010
Atakumosa East	76,105	38,945	37,160
Atakumosa West	68,350	34,859	33,491
Boluwaduro	70,954	36,045	34,909
Boripe	138,742	71,052	67,690
Ede North	83,818	42,282	41,536
Ede South	75,489	38,233	37,256
Egbedore	73,969	37,302	36,667
Ejigbo	132,515	67,437	65,078
Ife Central	167,204	88,403	78,801
Ife East	188,614	95,106	93,508
Ife North	153,274	75,852	76,422
Ife South	134,490	68,450	66,040
Ifedayo	37,508	19,227	18,281
Ifelodun	96,444	48,567	47,877
Ila	62,054	31,488	30,566
Ilesha East	105,416	52,721	52,695
Ilesha West	106,809	52,985	53,824
Irepodun	119,590	60,553	59,037
Irewole	142,806	71,730	71,076
Isokan	102,060	51,304	50,756
Iwo	191,348	96,419	94,929
Obokun	116,850	59,587	57,263
Odo-Otin	132,078	67,956	64,122
Ola-Oluwa	76,227	39,233	36,994
Olorunda	131,649	66,684	64,965
Oriade	148,379	75,213	73,166

LGA	Both Sexes	Male	Female
Orolu	102,832	52,790	50,042
Osogbo	155,507	78,395	77,112
Osun State	**3,416,959**	**1,734,149**	**1,682,810**

OYO

LGA	Both Sexes	Male	Female
Afijio	132,184	66,434	65,750
Akinyele	211,811	105,594	106,217
Atiba	168,246	84,266	83,980
Atigbo	109,965	56,747	53,218
Egbeda	283,643	137,527	146,116
Ibadan Central (Ibadan North East)	331,444	163,844	167,600
Ibadan North	308,119	152,608	155,511
Ibadan North West	154,029	75,410	78,619
Ibadan South West	266,457	130,334	136,123
Ibadan South West	283,098	139,622	143,476
Ibarapa Central	103,243	52,094	51,149
Ibarapa East	117,182	59,315	57,867
Ibarapa North	100,293	51,272	49,021
Ido	104,087	52,465	51,622
Irepo	121,240	62,601	58,639
Iseyin	255,619	129,268	126,351
Itesiwaju	127,391	65,820	61,571
Iwajowa	102,847	52,472	50,375
Kajola	200,528	101,188	99,340
Lagelu	148,133	74,220	73,913
Ogbomosho North	198,859	103,418	95,441
Ogbomosho South	100,379	50,862	49,517
Ogo Oluwa	65,198	33,403	31,795
Olorunsogo	81,339	41,795	39,544
Oluyole	203,461	102,371	101,090
Ona-Ara	265,571	130,615	134,956
Orelope	104,004	52,996	51,008
Ori Ire	149,408	76,465	72,943
Oyo East	124,095	62,147	61,948
Oyo West	136,457	68,897	67,560
Saki West	108,957	56,014	52,943
Saki West	273,268	138,677	134,591
Surulere	140,339	71,671	68,668
Oyo State	**5,580,894**	**2,802,432**	**2,778,462**

PLATEAU

LGA	Both Sexes	Male	Female
Barikin Ladi	179,805	90,913	88,892
Bassa	189,834	94,725	95,105
Bokkos	179,550	88,560	90,990
Jos East	88,301	44,980	43,321
Jos North	437,217	220,856	216,361
Jos South	311,392	157,067	154,325
Kanam	167,619	81,162	86,457
Kanke	124,268	61,376	62,892
Langtang North	142,316	70,203	72,113
Langtang South	105,173	53,111	52,062
Mangu	300,520	148,590	151,930
Mikang	96,388	47,584	48,804
Pankshin	190,114	95,376	94,738
Qua'an Pan	197,276	96,800	100,476
Riyon	131,778	66,248	65,530
Shendam	205,119	101,951	103,168
Wase	159,861	79,496	80,365
Plateau State	**3,206,531**	**1,598,998**	**1,607,533**

RIVERS

LGA	Both Sexes	Male	Female
Abua/Odual	282,410	145,243	137,167
Ahoada East	166,324	85,467	80,857
Ahoada West	249,232	127,906	121,326
Akuku Toru	161,103	82,949	78,454
Andoni	217,924	111,946	105,978
Asari-Toru	219,787	112,283	107,504
Bonny	214,983	116,340	98,643
Degema	249,467	128,041	121,426
Eleme	190,194	98,345	91,849
Emohua	210,057	102,634	98,423
Etche	249,939	127,869	122,070
Gokana	233,813	118,222	115,591
Ikwerre	188,930	97,575	91,355
Khana	292,924	147,315	145,609
Obia/Akpor	462,350	238,951	223,399
Ogba/Egbema/Ndoni	283,294	145,326	137,968
Ogu/Bolo	75.282	38,552	36,730

Okrika	222,285	113,962	108,323
Omumma	100,388	50,853	49,535
Opobe/Nkoro	152,833	77,556	75,277
Oyigbo	125,331	63,434	61,897
Port-Harcourt	538,558	280,703	257,855
Tai	120,308	61,554	58,754
Rivers State	**5,198,716**	**2,673,026**	**2,525,690**

SOKOTO

LGA	Both Sexes	Male	Female
Binji	104,274	52,949	51,325
Bodinga	174,302	87,844	86,458
Dange-Shuni	193,443	97,709	95,734
Gada	249,051	122,232	126,819
Goronyo	182,118	90,639	91,479
Gudu	95,400	48,125	47,275
Gwadabawa	231,569	116,300	115,269
Illela	150,133	74,949	75,184
Isa	150,268	73,474	76,794
Kebbe	123.154	62,338	60,816
Kware	134,084	66,778	67,306
Rabah	149,152	75,001	74,151
Sabon Birni	207,470	99,397	108,073
Shagari	156,907	79,438	77,469
Silame	104,601	53,091	51,510
Sokoto North	233,012	124,134	108,878
Sokoto South	197,686	103,207	94,479
Tambuwal	225,917	113,495	112,422
Tangaza	114,770	55,309	59,461
Tureta	68,414	34,567	33,847
Wamakko	179,246	91,466	87,780
Wurno	162,403	81,854	80,549
Yabo	115,302	59,417	55,885
Sokoto State	**3,702,676**	**1,863,713**	**1,838,963**

YOBE

LGA	Both Sexes	Male	Female
Bade	139,804	73,709	66,095
Bursari	109,692	56,381	53,311
Damaturu	87,706	48,361	39,345
Fika	136,736	69,175	67,567
Fune	301,954	150,896	151,058
Geidam	155,740	82,482	73,258
Gujba	129,797	72,310	57,487
Gulani	103,516	51,686	51,830
Jakusko	232,458	120,728	111,730
Karasuwa	105,514	55,385	50,129
Machina	60,994	31,771	29,223
Nangere	87,517	44,470	43,047
Nguru	150,699	80,827	69,872
Potiskun	204,866	105,388	99,478
Tarmua	77,667	40,612	37,055
Yunusari	125,940	64,918	61,022
Yunufari	110,739	55,935	54,804
Yobe State	**2,321,339**	**1,205,034**	**1,116,305**

ZAMFARA

LGA	Both Sexes	Male	Female
Anka	143,637	72,456	71,181
Bakura	187,141	92,369	94,772
Birnin Magaji	184,083	90,824	93,259
Bukkuyun	216,348	108,812	107,536
Bungudu	258,644	128,831	129,813
Gunmi	206,721	102,686	104,035
Gusau	383,712	198,682	185,030
Kaura Namoda	285,363	145,548	139,815
Maradun	207,563	106,403	101,160
Maru	293,141	146,920	146,221
Shinkafi	135,964	66,512	69,452
Talata Mafara	215,650	107,516	108,134
Tsafe	266,929	129,010	137,919
Zurmi	293,977	145,054	148,923
Zamfara State	**3,278,873**	**1,641,623**	**1,637,250**

FCT ABUJA

LGA	Both Sexes	Male	Female
Abaji	58,642	28,860	29,782
Abuja Municipal	776,298	415,951	360,347
Bwari	229,274	115,346	113,928
Gwagwalada	158,618	80,182	78,436
Kuje	97,233	49,420	47,813
Kwali	86,174	43,413	42,761
FCT Abuja	**1,406,239**	**733,172**	**673,067**

Issued under my hand this 2nd day of February, 2009.

UMARU MUSA YAR'ADUA, GCFR

President of the Federal Republic of Nigeria

Table 3.4: States and Their Dates of Creation in Nigeria

S/N	State	Date Created	Capital	Preceding	EntryKm²
1	Abia	27 Aug. 1991	Umuahia	Imo State	6,320
2	Adamawa	27 Aug. 1991	Yola	Gongola State	36,917
3	Akwa Ibom	23 Sept. 1987	Uyo	Cross River State	7,081
4	Anambra	27 Aug. 1991	Awka	*old(Anambra State	4,844
5	Bauchi	3 Feb. 1976	Bauchi	North-Eastern State	45,837
6	Bayeka	1 Oct. 1996	Yenagoa	Rivers State	10,773
7	Benue	3 Feb. 1976	Makurdi	Benue-Plateau State	34,059
8	Borno	3 February,	Maiduguri	North-Eastern State	70,898
9	Cross River	27 May 1976	Calabar	Eastern Region; previously known as South-Eastern State	10,156
10	Delta	27 Aug. 1991	Asaba	Bendel State	17,698
11	Ebonyi	1 Oct. 1996	Abakaliki	Enugu State and Abia State	5,670
12	Edo	27 Aug. 1991	Benin City	Bendel State	17,800
13	Ekiti	1 Oct. 1996	Ado-Ekiti	Ondo State	6,353
14	Enugu	27 Aug. 1991	Enugu	*old(Anambra State	7,161
15	Gombe	1 Oct. 1996	Gombe	Bauchi State	18,768
16	Imo	3 Feb. 1976	Owerri	East Central State	5,100
17	Jigawa	27 Aug. 1991	Dutse	Kano State	23,154
18	Kaduna	27 May, 1967	Kaduna	Northern Region;previously known as North-Central State	46,053
19	Kano	27 May 1967	Kano	Northern Region	20,131
20	Katsina	23 Sept. 1987	Katsina	Kaduna State	24,192
21	Kebbi	27 Aug. 1991	Birnin Kebbi	Sokoto State	36,800
22	Kogi	27 Aug. 1991	Lokoja	Kwara State; Benue State	29,833
23	Kwara	27 Aug. 1967	Ilorin	Northern Region; previously known as West Central State	36,825

#	State	Date	Capital	Created from	Area
24	Lagos	27 May, 1967	Ikeja	Province of Lagos + colony	3,345
25	Nasarawa	1 Oct. 1996	Lafia	Plateau State	27,117
26	Niger	3 Feb. 1976	Minna	North-Western State	76,363
27	Ogun	3 Feb. 1976	Abeokuta	Western State	16,762
28	Ondo	3 Feb. 1976	Akure	Western State	15,500
29	Osun	27 Aug. 1991	Oshogbo	Oyo State	9,251
30	Oyo	3 Feb. 1976	Ibadan	Western State	28,454
31	Plateau	3 Feb. 1976	Jos	Benue-Plateau State	30,913
32	Rivers	27 May 1967	Port Harcourt	Eastern Region	11,077
33	Sokoto	3 Feb. 1976	Sokoto	North-Western State	25,973
34	Taraba	27, Aug., 1991	Jalingo	Gongola State	54,473
35	Yobe	27 Aug. 1991	Damaturu	Borno State	45,502
36	Zamfara	1 Oct., 1996	Gusau	Sokoto State	39,762
37	FCT Abuja	3 Feb. 1976	Abuja	Benue-Plateau, North-Central and North-Western States	7,315

CHAPTER 4

Know Your Continent - Africa

Africa second largest of earth's seven continents, covering 23 percent of the world's total land area and 13 percent of the world's population. Africa straddles the equator and most of its area lies within the tropics. It is bounded by the Atlantic Ocean on the West, the Indian Ocean and the Red Sea on the East, and the Mediterranean Sea on the North. In the Northeastern corner of the continent, Africa is connected with Asia by the Sinai Peninsula.

Africa is a land of great diversity: lush green forest, cast grassy plains: barren deserts, tall mountains: some of the mightiest rivers on earth: diverse people with a wide range of cultures and backgrounds and hundreds of different languages: small villages where daily life remains largely the same a it has been for hundreds of years as well as sprawling cities with sky scrapers, modern economies, and a mix of international cultural influences.

During the last 500 years, however, Africa became increasingly dominated by European traders and colonisers. European traders sent millions of Africans to work as slaves on colonial plantations in North America, South America, The Caribbean. Europeans also sought

Africa's wealth of raw materials to fuel their industries. In the late 19th century European powers seized and colonised virtually all of Africa.

There are 53 different African countries, including the 47 nations of the mainland and the 6 surrounding island nations. The continent is commonly divided along the lines of the Sahara, the world's largest, which cuts a huge swath through the northern half of the continent. The countries north of the Sahara make up the region of North Africa, while the region south of the desert is known as sub-Saharan Africa. Sub-Saharan Africa is sometimes referred to as "Black Africa" but this designation is not very helpful, given the ethnic diversity of the entire continent. North Africa consists of the countries of Algeria, Egypt, Libya, Morocco, Sudan, and Tunisia. Sub-Saharan Africa is generally subdivided into the regions of West Africa, East Africa, Central Africa and Southern Africa. West Africa consists of Benin, Burkina Faso, Cameroun, Chad, Cote D' Ivoire, Ghana, Guinea, Guinea-Bissau, Liberia, Mali, Mauritania, Niger, Nigeria, Senegal, Sierra Leone, The Gambia, and Togo. East Africa consists of Burundi, Djibouti, Eritrea, Ethiopia, Kenya, Malawi, Mozambique, Rwanda, Somalia, Tanzania, and Uganda. Central Africa consists of Angola, Central African Republic, Democratic Republic of Congo, and Zambia. Southern Africa consists of Botswana, Lesotho, Namibia, South Africa, Swaziland, and Zimbabwe. The island nations located off the coast of Africa are Cape Verde, and Sao Tome and Principe in the Atlantic Ocean: and Comoros, Madagascar: Mauritius and Seychelles in the Indian Ocean. The population of African countries as at 2006 is given in Table 4.1.

The African countries cover 30 million sq. Km (12 million sq. mi), including its adjacent islands. It stretches 8,000km (5,000 miles) from its northernmost point, Ra'sal Abyad in Tunisia, to its southernmost tips Cape Agulhas in South Africa. The maximum width of the continent, measured from the tip of Cape Verde in Senegal, in the West to Raas Xaafun (Ras Hufun) in Somalia, in the East is 7,500 km (4,700mi). The highest point on the continent is the perpetually snow capped Kilimanjaro (5,895m/19,341ft) in Tanzania and the lowest is Lake Asal (153m/502ft below area level) in Djibouti.

Africa is surrounded by oceans and seas: the Atlantic Ocean on the West, the Indian Ocean on the East, the Red Sea on the Northeast and the Mediterranean Sea on the North. Madagascar, the fourth largest island in the world, lies off the Southern coast. Other offshore islands include the Madeira Islands, Canary Islands, and Cape-Verde Islands, Sao Tome and Principe; and Bioko, off the Western coast, and the Comoros Islands, Seychelles, Mascarene Islands, and Socotra, off the Eastern coast.

Highlands

The highest elevations in Africa are found in the various ranges of East Africa. After Kilimanjaro, the next highest peaks are Mount Kenya (5, 199m/17,057ft) North of Kilimanjaro in central Kenya: Marguerite Peak (5,109m/16, 762ft) in the Ruwenzori Range on the border between Uganda and the Democratic Republic of the Congo (DRC), Ras Dashen (4, 620m/ 15,157ft) in the Ethiopian highlands of Northern Ethiopia; Mount Meru (4,565m/14,977ft), close to Kilimanjaro in Tanzania, and mount Elgon (4,321m/14,177ft) on the Kenya- Uganda border.

Africa's other major mountainous regions occur at the Northern and Southern fringes of the continent. The Atlas Mountains, a system of high degree, extend for 2,200km (1,400mi) across Morocco, Algeria, and Tunisia, roughly parallel to the Northern coast. These ranges enclose a number of broad inland basins and plateaus. In the West, the high (or grand) Atlas contains Toubkal (4,165m/13,665ft), the highest peak of the system. Towards the East, the Atlas consists of two parallel ranges: the Tell Atlas to the North and the Saharan Atlas to the South.

In the Southern Africa, the U-shaped Great Escarpment extends 5,000km (3,000mi) along the coast from Angola to Mozambique (an escarpment is a ridge that is steep on one side and slopes down gently on the other). The Drakensberg Mountains form the most pronounced relief of the Great Escarpment, rising to 3,482m (11,424ft) at the Thabana Ntlenyana in Lesotho.

Cameroun Mountains is the highest peak in West Africa at 4,095m (13,435ft). To the North, isolated highlands occur in the desert land of the Sahara, including the Hagar mountains in Southern Algeria and the Tibesti in Northern Chad.

Great Rift Valley

The Great Rift Valley is one of the most distinctive features of African topography. Formed where earth crust is being pulled apart by the action of convection currents beneath the surface, rift valleys are long, deep valleys bounded by parallel faults, or fractures in earth crust. The great Rift Valley system begins in Syria, in the Middle East, and extends Southward, down the length of the Red Sea. It enters Africa at the Afar Depression on the coast of

Eritrea and Djibouti, and winds some 5,600km (3,500mi) to the coast of Southern Mozambique. In its middle section, it breaks into two major branches, the Eastern Rift Valley and the Western Rift Valley. The Rift Valley is flanked by towering escarpments of up to 1,000 m (3,000ft) in Southern Ethiopia, (4,900ft) along the Eastern Rift in central Kenya and 1,300m (4,300ft) in the Northern part of the Western Rift, along the DRC's border with Uganda, Rwanda, and Burundi. The Southern extremities of the Rift system are much less spectacular in size and appearance.

Several major lakes, typically long and narrow, are located on the floors of the Western and Eastern rift valleys. The Western rift contains Lake Albert, Lake Edward, and Lake Kivu to the North, Lake Tanganyika in the middle, and Lake Malawi (Lake Nyasa) to the South. The lakes of the Eastern rift tend to be smaller and include Lake Naivasha, lake Natron and the Southern part of Lake Turkana.

The Sahara is the world largest desert. It stretches from the Atlantic Ocean to the red sea and from the Mediterranean Sea and Atlas Mountains Southward for 2,000km (1,000mi) until it merges imperceptibly into the semi desert Sahel region. Most of the desert consists of extensive plains covered with loose gravel and boulders called reg. The rest of the desert is made up of areas of shifting sand dunes, called erg, interspersed with stretches of bare, rocky areas called Hamada.

The Namib and Kalahari deserts of Southern Africa are much smaller than the Sahara. The Namib Desert stretches along the Atlantic coast for 1,500km (930mi) from Southern Angola along the entire length of Namibia, and into

Western South Africa. The nearby Kalahari Desert, in Botswana, Namibia, and South Africa, is semi arid in the centre of the Kalahari Basin.

Source – Microsoft Corporation

Lakes, Rivers, And Wetlands

The water systems of Africa are extremely diverse, a reflection of the continent's great range of climate and physical geography. These systems vary from region and from season and year as well.

Africa has several of the world's greatest rivers. The Congo, which alone accounts for some 38 percent of the continent's discharge into the ocean, drains an area of more than 4.1 million sq. km (1.6 million sq. mi), ranking second only to South America's Amazon river in terms of discharge and size of drainage basin. The Nile, which extends for 6,695 km (4,160mi), is the world's longest river; it occupies the fourth largest drainage basin. Other important rivers include the Niger in West Africa and the Zambezi in Southern Africa.

Africa's river systems reflect the continents' unique physical geography. One-third of its area consists of inland basins, such as Lake Chad and Kalahari (Okavango) basins, where rivers and streams never reach the ocean. Other major river systems, notably the Nile, Niger, and Congo rivers have large inland deltas in midcourse, indicating that the upper portions of these river's drainage basins were also landlocked at some point. Several major rivers including the Congo, Zambezi, and Orange, pass through narrow valleys and drop sharply as they cross escarpments fringing the continent.

In its lower course, the Congo drops 270m (886ft) through a series of 30 rapids and waterfalls. River courses such as this provide ideal condition for hydroelectric power generation. Africa has about 40 percent of the world's hydroelectric potential, but only a small proportion has been developed.

Africa's many lakes have diverse characteristic. They include deep lakes of tectonics origin (such as lakes Malawi and Tanganyika in East Africa) and shallow lakes located at the centre of drainage basins (including Lake Chad in West Africa). Lake Victoria in East Africa, is the world's second deepest lake and third largest by volume of water. Africa's natural lakes have quite distinct ecologies: lakes located close to each other often vary significantly in both abundance and types of fish and plant species. Most lakes contribute significantly to their regional economies, particularly as a source of fish.

Wetlands area plays a vital hydrological and ecological role in Africa. They trap and slow seasonal floods, deepening the magnitude of floods downstream and spreading out peak flows over several weeks or months. The delay and extension of flood peaks can facilitate downstream fishing and irrigation, especially in areas with an extended dry season. Wetlands also provide habitat for numerous species of animals and plants, many of them unique to these ecosystems. Wetlands near the edge of the Sahara provide vital staging grounds for migratory birds preparing to cross the desert. Wetlands also trap and hold silt carried by rivers, creating fertile alluvial soils that may be used to grow crops such as rice, cotton and vegetables. However agricultural development schedule taking advantage of the presence of both fertile soil and water pose a threat to many wetlands.

Botswana's Okavango Delta is one of Africa's largest and most unique wetlands. The Okavango River, with its source in the highlands of Angola, forms a huge, swampy inland delta as it approaches the Kalahari Desert. During the annual floods, the swamp doubles in size. Although it has several outlets virtually all of the water entering the Okavango Delta evaporates or it's absorbed into the sandy subsurface. The Okavango supports a rich indigenous flora and fauna, and attracts huge number of migratory wildlife during the season. Like many others, this vital and sensitive wetland ecosystem is threatened by the growth of ranching and tourism, and by proposals to divert water for irrigation and other uses.

Lying between latitudes 37° North and 35° South, Africa has virtually the same climate zone in the Northern hemisphere and they are arranged symmetrically on either side of the equator. The zones are determined mainly by latitude, except in the East where highlands greatly modify the climate. Africa is the most tropical of the continents: only its Northern and Southern extremes are directly influenced by mid-latitude westerly winds and are considered to have temperate climates.

Climatic Zones

Most of Africa lies between the tropic of cancer (in the North) and the tropic of Capricorn (in the South) and has high temperature through out the year. The amounts, duration and seasonal distribution of rainfall are therefore the most important factor differentiating its climates. Africa has six types of climatic zones: tropical wet, tropical summer rainfall, semiarid, arid, and highland and Mediterranean.

Tropical Wet

Tropical wet climates, also called equatorial climates, occur close to the equator in West and Central Africa, and in Eastern Madagascar. Rainfall is high, typically exceeding 1,500mm (60in) per year and 3,200mm (130 in) in some places. Rainfall occurs in every month and many areas experience especially rainy periods in the spring and in the fall. Temperatures remain high throughout the year, averaging more than 27°C (81°F) annually, and rarely falling below 21°C (70°F).

Tropical Summer Rainfall

Tropical summer rainfall climates, also known as tropical savannah climates occur North and South of the tropical wet zones in much of West Africa and southern Africa and most of Madagascar. This climate zone is marked by a well-defined dry season of three to eight months. Annual rainfall is usually between 500 and 1,500mm (20 and 60 in), although limited areas have considerably more, for example; Freetown, Sierra Leone, averages 3,800mm (150 in) per year. The tropical summer rainfall is the transitional zone between tropical wet and semiarid zones, so there is progressive decline, moving pole ward, in total rainfall and the duration of rainfall. Areas with longer rainy season tend to have two rainy periods separated by a short dry spell, while areas with a shorter rainy season have single rainy period.

Temperature ranges in the tropical summer rainfall zone are slightly higher than in the tropical wet zone, and increase with distance from the equator. In the Northern section of this zone, daily high temperature average more than 30°C(90°F) over the course of the year. Temperatures in the Southern and Eastern sections of this zone tend to be cooler because of higher altitudes.

Semiarid And Arid

Surrounding the tropical summer rainfall zone are areas of semiarid and then arid climates in North central Africa, East central Africa, and Southern Africa. The semiarid or hot steppe, zone has a short rainy season of up to three months with about 250 to 500mm (10 to 20 in) of rain per year. Precipitation is unreliable and scarce, creating difficult conditions for plant growth. Temperatures vary in the semiarid zones with average daily highs ranging from 25° to 36° C (77° to 97°F) Africa's arid desert regions receive little rainfall. Although classified as hot deserts, these regions have significant annual variation in temperature and extreme fluctuations in temperature over the course of a day. In the Sahara, day time summer temperature can exceed 50°C (120°F), and winter night time temperature can drop below freezing.

Highland And Mediterranean

Tropical climates are common in much of East Africa. Temperatures in the highlands of Ethiopia and Kenya average 16°C to 21°C (60°F to 70°F), on average about 5 Celsius degrees (9 Fahrenheit degrees) cooler than the lower plateau areas of Kenya, Uganda, and Tanzania. In most parts of the world, higher elevations receive higher levels of precipitation but the highlands of east Africa are exceptions, experiencing rather low levels of rainfalls. However, the highest mountains and the Southeastern flank of the Ethiopian plateau receive greater precipitation on their windward slopes.

The coastlands of the cape region of South Africa and the North African coast from Morocco to Tunisia have Mediterranean climates. These areas have mild, rainy winters followed by a summer when conditions are warm and dry. They receive between 250 to 1,000mm (10 to 40 in) of rainfall per year.

People Of Africa

Africa was the birthplace of the human species between 8 million and 5 million years ago. Today, the vast majority of its inhabitants are of indigenous origin. People across the continent are remarkably diverse by just about any measure: they speak a vast number of different languages, practice hundreds of distinct religions, live in types of dwellings and engage in a wide range of economic activities.

Over the centuries, people from other parts of the world have migrated to Africa and settled there. Historically, Arabs have been the most numerous immigrants. Starting in the 7th century AD, they crossed into North Africa from the Middle East, bringing the religion of Islam with them. A later movement of Arab into the East and Central Africa occurred in the 19th century. Europeans first settled in Africa in the mid-17th century near the Cape of Good Hope, at the Southern end of the continent. More Europeans immigrated during the subsequent colonial periods, particularly to present-day South Africa, Zimbabwe and Algeria. South Asians also arrived during colonial times. Their descendents often referred to as

Indians, are found largely in Uganda, Kenya, Tanzania, and South Africa.

In 2008, 955 million people or about 13 percent of the world's population lived in Africa. The most populous countries are Nigeria, Egypt, Ethiopia and the Democratic Republic of Congo (DRC). Distribution of the population is highly uneven. Some parts of the continent, particularly the vast Sahara have few permanent residents. Others rank among the world's most densely populated areas, notably the Nile valley of Egypt, the Atlantic coastal stretch from Cote d'Ivoire to Cameroun, Rwanda, Burundi, and South Africa's province of KwaZulu-Natal. Overall, Africa's population density is 32 persons per sq. km (83 persons per sq. mi).

Africa's Languages

The number of distinctive languages spoken in Africa is open to debate. Some experts put the number at around 2,000, while others count more than 3,000. Virtually, all of these languages originated in Africa. The most widely spoken indigenous African language is Swahili, spoken by nearly 50 million Africans, followed by Hausa and Yoruba, each with more than 20 million speakers. Several languages have only a few thousand speakers. Scholars generally recognise four African language families, Niger-Congo, Nilo-Saharan, and Khoisan.

Religion

The first world religion to reach Africa was Judaism, which spread into Egypt sometime during the 2nd millennium BC. Subsequently, Jewish people may have converted various Berber communities to the West. In addition, during the 1st century BC Jewish migrants crossed the Red Sea from the Arabian Peninsula and settled in the highlands of what is now Ethiopia. Over time, they won converts from the local population and eventually formed a distinctive Jewish community called Beta Israel (referred to derogatory as Falashas in Ethiopia).

During the first centuries AD Christianity spread across North Africa, more by conversion than migration. In Egypt, the Christian sect of Monophysitism gained pre-eminence, and Egyptian Monophysites became known as Coptic. Christianity spread South to Nubia, and reached Abyssinia during the 4th century, becoming the state religion of the kingdom of Aksum and subsequent Ethiopian states. Catholicism prevailed over rival Christian sects in Northwestern Africa with the help of Saint Augustine, an Algerian and one of the framers of western theology.

In 639 AD, Islam began its march across North Africa. For most part, even though Islam was brought by conquering armies, conversion was mostly voluntary. Converts were quickly won in Northwestern Africa, where many people saw Islam as a vibrant spiritual and material alternative to a decaying Christian world. Scattered catholic communities did, however, manage to survive in North Africa into the 15th century. Conversion to Islam moved slowly in Nubia and in Egypt, where the Coptic Church is still strong.

In the 8th century Arab merchants brought Islam to coastal communities along the horn of Africa, and the religion subsequently spread inland to other peoples, notably the Somali. In the 12th century, and possibly earlier Islam gained adherents farther south along the Indian Ocean coast in what is now Kenya and Tanzania.

In the mid-19th century, European missionaries reintroduced Christianity to Africa, and the process of winning converts picked up speed during the colonial era. Virtually all of the major denominations of Christianity, and many of the minor ones, established mission stations in Africa, leading to an intricate pattern of religion denominations. Africans found conversion to Christianity attractive because the missionaries offered health service and educational opportunities for their children.

However, Christian missionaries made little headway in Islamic strongholds and the continent therefore became divided between an overwhelming Islamic North and a more Christian South roughly speaking, latitude 10° North serves as the dividing line from West Africa until East Africa, where it swings South of the equator to about 8° South. While Christians are few in number North of the line, Muslims are more common to the South of it. In Malawi and Mozambique, for example, 15 to 20 percent of the population count themselves as Muslims. Violence sometimes erupts between Islam and Christianity along the dividing line. This has been an ongoing social issue in Ethiopia for 800 years. Since 1970 Chad and the Sudan have seen ongoing strife and civil wars between the Islamic North and Christian-indigenous South. Sectarian violence has also occurred in Nigeria since the late 1990s. For the most part, however, the two religions are not in competition with one another and the continental dividing seems unlikely to change.

Education

Africans value education and all governments see improving educational access and quality as essential to national economic and political development. Despite scarce finances, many countries have made note worthy achievements in raising literacy rates in recent decades. Adult literacy rates of 70 percent or more are characteristic of East, Central, and Southern Africa, except, notably, in Somalia, Angola, Ethiopia and Mozambique. Gains have been less impressive in West Africa: Many countries still have literacy rates below 60 percent, and the rates in Niger, Burkina Faso and Sierra Leone are among the worlds lowest. Cameroun, Ghana, and Nigeria are notable exceptions, with particularly high literacy rates. Libya, Tunisia, and Algeria in North Africa have rates of 90 percent or higher. Females have significantly lower literacy rates than males across most of Africa.

Compulsory School attendance, starting at either 6 or 7 years of age and lasting until the ages of 11 to 16, is now universal in Africa. In many instances, education is free. A major obstacle to universal education is the problem of providing enough teachers, schools, and classroom materials to meet children's needs, especially in remote rural areas. Huge national debts, the economic austerity measures designed to eliminate them, and military expenditures have all limited the funds that most countries have available to devote to education. Another obstacle to ensuring that all children receive education is the fact that they are still an important part of the workforce across Africa. They provide childcare, work farms and herds, and perform a range of other menial jobs, such as drawing water and collecting firewood.

Parents may also lack the financial means to send their children to school, or may be forced to choose which ones can go and which ones cannot. Boys are usually given preference over girls in access to education and they typically stay in school much longer. The rationale for this is based on future income-earning potential. As matters currently stand, males have access to more and better paying jobs than females. Deteriorating economic conditions have actually led the income-earning and literacy gaps between males and females to widen even more.

Universities have space for only a small fraction of secondary school graduates and competition to secure admittance is intense. Those who are admitted are not guaranteed a good education, however. University libraries are often poorly stocked and, most critically, lack up-to-date scientific journals. Computers are few and Internet access rare. Most campuses were built in the 1950s and 1960s and have deteriorated, the more so because of limited funds for maintenance. The quality of higher education is also affected by frequent student protests over issues ranging from poor living conditions to politics. On many occasions governments have responded with force and closed campuses for considerable periods of time. While faculties are usually of high quality, with many members having been trained in Europe and North America, the conditions severely constrain what they can do. As a result, many look outside Africa for employment, which contributes significantly to Africa's brain drain.

Mining

Africa plays a very important role in the global mineral economy, producing about three-quarters for the world's cobalt; half of the global supply of platinum, chromium, and diamonds; approximately one-third of all gold, manganese, and uranium; one-fifth of all bauxite; and one-tenth of the world's petroleum. Minerals account for at least half of export earnings in 12 African countries, and 90 percent or more of exports in Angola, Nigeria, Algeria, Libya, and Zambia. The countries of the Sahel and East Africa, where mineral production is unimportant, are notable exceptions.

North Africa is one the world's major centres of oil production. Libya, Algeria, and Egypt are among Africa's top producers of crude petroleum. Algeria has vast reserves of natural gas as well. North Africa is also rich in phosphate deposits and production, more so, being a leader in world output. Of lesser significance in the region are coal, iron ore, uranium, platinum, lead, zinc, and cobalt.

West and Central Africa also contain significant oil reserves. Nigeria is Africa's top petroleum producer. Angola, Gabon, and the Republic of the Congo are other important oil-producing countries. West and Central Africa also possess some of the world's most significant sources of cobalt, manganese, potash, bauxite, and copper. Guinea has about one-third of the world's reserve of bauxite, the commercial source of aluminium. Other minerals of economic significance are iron ore, gold, diamonds, tin, uranium, phosphate, columbite, and titanium.

Southern Africa is one of the world's richest sources of gold, diamonds, and several rare metals. South Africa has the largest and most diverse mineral economy, and is a leading producer of gold and of uncut diamonds. Zimbabwe is also an important producer of gold, while Botswana and Namibia are important producers of diamonds. Other important minerals produced in Southern Africa include chromium, cobalt, antimony, uranium, lithium, nickel, manganese asbestos, platinum, titanium, and vanadium.

The economies of African countries that are heavily dependent on one principal mineral export are seriously affected by price declines in the world market. Recent decades have seen destabilising shifts in the price of Zambia's copper, Guinea's bauxite, and Togo's phosphate. However, of recent, the demand for copper has increased, leading to increase in the market price of copper.

Energy

Wood from trees and shrub is still the most important source of domestic fuel in Africa. Use of coal and petroleum is limited to urban centres, modern factories, and power plants. In 2003, seventy-nine percent of the electricity generated in Africa was produced by burning coal and other fossil fuels.

The most promising source of energy in Africa is hydroelectric power generation. The continent's many large rivers give it a vast hydro-power potential that has barely been tapped. Several major installations have been constructed since 1960, including the Aswan High Dam on the Nile River, the Akosombo Dam on the Volta River, and the Kariba Dam and Cabora Bassea Dam on the Zambezi River.

In 2003 African hydroelectric plants produced eighteen percent of the electricity generated in Africa.

West Africa To The 1870s

From the 17th to the 19th century in Sub-Saharan West Africa – from the Senegal river estuary in the West to Cameroun in the East and as far South as Angola – Political and economic life was dominated by the demands of the European – controlled Atlantic slave trade. By the late 18th century the scale of this trade had reached unprecedented heights, with up to 100,000 captives exported every year. The wars that generated this traffic dominated life in the interior. States with standing armies became more centralised and more powerful, dominating smaller, village – based communities. For the most part, European presence was confined to coastal fortresses, which were fortified against European rivals rather than local Africans. Coastal African rulers tolerated the European presence because the European fortresses provided useful trading links that strengthened their positions against their own African rivals.

Two important developments occurred in 18th century West Africa that presaged large–scale change in the 19th century. First, by the mid 18th century a rise in Islamic reformist zeal led to several jihads and the establishment of new Islamic states in Fouta Djallon (in what is now Guinea) and Fouta Toro (in Senegal). Second, in the 1780s and 1790s Britain helped freed slaves from Britain and North America establish settlements in the British territory of Sierra Leone. The Islamic states of Fouta Djallon and

Fouta Toro served as inspirations for larger 19th – century West African Jihads, while the colony of Sierra Leone was symbolic of the emerging abolitionist movement that would eventually bring an end to the Atlantic slave trade.

Jihads And New States In 19TH Century West Africa

West African Islamic reformist ideas of the late 18th and early 19th centuries were spread by Fulani people, who had played a prominent role in the earlier jihads for Fouta Djallon and Fouta Toro. The Fulani – largely Muslim cattle herders who lived in the savannah lands from Senegal to Cameroun – typically lived in peace among farming population. However, in the Hausa region of what is now Northern Nigeria, the Fulani became estranged from what they regarded as the corrupt rule of the nominally Muslim Hausa aristocracy. They particularly resented the Hausa's heavy taxation of their cattle. The Fulani were therefore very receptive to the reformist teachings of Muslim scholar Usman dan Fodio, who had begun his preaching as a young man in the 1770s in the Hausa city-state of Gobir.

By the early 1800s, Usman had accumulated a considerable following. In 1804, the ruler of Gobir sent his cavalry to capture or kill Usman, but the force was defeated by Usman's followers. This military action sparked a spontaneous revolutionary movement among Fulani and other oppressed Muslims across the whole of Hausa land. Within four years most of the Hausa city-states had fallen to the Jihad. After Usman's death in 1817, his brother Abdullahi and son Muhammad Bello united the Hausa states into a single Islamic empire, with its capital at Sokoto. By the time of Muhammad Bello's death in 1837 this Sokoto Caliphate stretched across the whole of Northern Nigeria and was the largest West African state since 16th century Songhai. Islam and *Sharia* (Islamic law) made up the unifying elements in what was otherwise a federation of semi-autonomous emirates.

Literacy became widespread and, with an end to interstate Hausa wars, trade flourished. Those who benefited least were the Hausa peasantry, who had in effect changed one oppressive master for another.

Fulani pastoralists tried to extend the Jihad into Bornu, but they were resisted by Muhammad el-Kanemi, a religious and military leader from Kanem. Although the state lost control of its Eastern Hausa provinces, Bornu retained its independence under a new dynasty set up by el-Kanemi's son Umar.

West of Sokoto, Usuman dan Fodio's revolution inspired further Fulani-led Jihads and political change. On the upper Niger River, a Jihad was led by Umar Tal, a Muslim preacher from Fouta Toro. In the Fouta Djallon region, he built up an army and equipped it with firearms, bought in exchange for captives on the coast. From 1855 to 1862 Umar's army captured the Bambara states of Kaarta and Segou, and the Fulani state of Macina. He thus created what was known as the Tukolor Empire, which stretched from Fouta Djallon to Timbuktu. Following Umar's death in 1864, Tukolor was weakened by internal revolts and was conquered by the French in 1893.

South of Tukolor, in what is now Guinea, military leader Samory Toure conquered and united the states of the Dyula people in the 1860s, creating the powerful

Mandinka state. Unlike some of his contemporary state-builders, Samory was not a religious preacher and Mandinka was not a reformist state as such. Nevertheless, he used Islam to unite the nation, promoting Muslim education and basing his rule upon the *sharia*. Samory's professional army was the real strength of what had become a Mandinka empire by the 1880s. As such it provided one of the major forces of resistance to French conquest in the final decades of the century.

Abolition Of The Slave Trade

How the Atlantic slave trade came to be abolished has been the subject of ongoing historical debate. The traditional view argued by British historians for much of the 20th century was that the abolition of the slave trade was the result of a humanitarian campaign spearheaded by a handful of prominent British philanthropists. This view was challenged in the mid-20th century by historians who argued that it was hard economics, not humanitarian concerns that ended the slave trade. According to this view, by 1800 colonial plantations were declining in profitability, while the spread of industry in Britain was becoming increasing profitable, making the slave trade unnecessary.

Many historians now agree that the complete story of abolition was in fact very much more complex than either of these positions. Both economics and philanthropy were involved, though which was the more powerful force remains a subject of debate. Another factor, often overlooked, was African opposition to slavery, both in the form of slave rebellions in the Caribbean and resistance within Africa itself.

Coastal And Forest Regions

African powers had not been consulted in the official European ban on slave trading, and states in many areas, eager to acquire European firearms, continued to supply the European, American, and Brazilian ships that evaded the ban. One such area was the Yoruba lands of present day Southern Nigeria, which had not previously been a great supplier of captives for sale into slavery. But when the Fulani Jihad spread southward from Sokoto in the 1820s, it destabilized the Yoruba state of Oyo and prompted warfare across the whole of Yoruba land. Increasing numbers of Yoruba war captives were subsequently transported to the Lagos lagoon for export as slaves. This provided the British with the excuse to seize control of Lagos in 1851 in the name of suppressing the slave trade. In reality it provided the British with a colonial foothold. They declared Lagos a colony in 1861 and over the next 40 years, gradually extended British control over the whole of what was to become the colony of Nigeria.

The Kingdom of Dahomey, in what is now Southern Benin, used the Yoruba wars as an opportunity to break free of Oyo domination and assert its independence. With the backing of a large standing army, Dahomey's kings built a highly efficient and powerful centralised state. Dahomey's wealth was originally derived from the slave trade, but as the trade was suppressed in the mid-19th century, the king turned to the exploitation of the region's numerous oil palm plantations. Palm production that was not directly controlled by the state was taxed in a highly efficient manner. When the French took over the territory at the end of the century, they estimated that it contained 40 million palm trees.

The Ashanti Kingdom, in what is now Ghana, was the largest and most powerful West African forest state throughout most of the 19th century. Ashanti derived its wealth from the production of gold dust, which it traded with British, Danish and Dutch traders on the coast. Consequently, the region was known to Europeans as "the Gold Coast." The British sought to control the gold trade, and allied themselves with the coastal Fante people– bitter rivals of the Ashanti, to keep Ashanti from monopolising the trade. Ashanti and British forces clashed in the mid – 1820s, but signed a peace treaty in 1826. In the 1840s the British bought a string of Danish forts along the coast and in 1872 purchased the Dutch fort of Elmina. This left Britain as the sole European power in the area. The king of Ashanti challenged the rising colonial power by invading the British-held coast in 1873, sparking the second Ashanti-British War. A British counter invasion in 1874 penetrated deep into the Ashanti heartland where British forces sacked the Ashanti capital of Kumasi. The British withdrew, but Ashanti had been fatally weakened and finally fell to British forces in 1896.

To the West, at the mouth of the Senegal River, the French held the trading towns of Saint Louis, Goree, Dakar, and Rufisque. These were important bases for access to trade in gum Arabic (used in dying cloth) and groundnuts from the interior. The inland Wolof state of Fouta Toro imposed taxes on most of this trade, however, and in response the French sent an army up the Senegal River valley in the

1850s. By 1858 the army had defeated the Wolof and established a protectorate over the region. In the process the French clashed with the jihad army of Umar Tal, which prompted him to turn East, toward the upper Niger River, where he founded the Tukolor Empire.

Over the course of the 19th century, Sierra Leone grew rapidly, as the British transported freed African captives from all over West Africa to the colony. These mixed groups of Africans communicated in Creole (or Krio), a mixture of English and African languages, and they were known collectively as Creoles. Starting in the 1820s groups of freed African Americans began settling to the East of Sierra Leone in a region they named Liberia. These Americo-Libarians established Liberia as an independent nation in 1847.

Conquest Of A Continent

In 1877 Anglo-American explorer Henry Morton Stanley emerged at the mouth of the Congo River, completing an arduous, three-year transcontinental trek and proving the Congo's navigability for thousands of kilometres above the rapids near its mouth. Ambitious Europeans, led by King Leopold II of Belgium, recognized the river as a major potential trading artery. By the early 1880s, Belgium and France had competing claims to territories on either side of lower Congo. Territorial acquisition quickly became competitive and strategic, as Europe's major powers decided that their future economic prosperity depended on their seizing as much of the continent for themselves as possible. The biggest players were Britain, France, Belgium, and Germany, with Spain and Italy playing lesser roles, and Portugal maintaining its claims to its long-standing colonies. The process was already well under way by the time the European powers met at the Berlin West Africa Conference of 1884 – 1885 to lay down the ground rules of the Scramble. The principal of these was that European claimants to any part of Africa had to prove their presence in the area by getting the signed agreement of a local Africa ruler or – if that was not possible or convenient – by military conquest.

Europeans frequently tricked illiterate African rulers into signing documents under false pretences. For example, in 1888 Ndebele king Lobengula inadvertently gave British businessman Cecil Rhodes and his private mining company the right to take over the whole of what is now Zimbabwe. The British government ignored Lobengula's subsequent protests and approved Rhode's colonisation of the country. Some African rulers, more experienced in European ways, willingly agreed to "protection" before the arrival of European military forces, and in this way managed to obtain some concessions. Lozi King Lewanika achieved better treatment for Lozi than the rest of what is now Zambia by agreeing to an 1889 British treaty of protection which left him with some power and kept the British from seizing Lozi land.

European armies eventually occupied most of the continent, brutally conquering most African states that resisted. African powers lost virtually every conflict for two main reasons: the age-old principle of divide-and – conquer and the superior weaponry of the European armies. Europeans were able to play one African ruler against another because a ruler's first duty to his people was to protect them from their traditional rivals or enemies. Up to this point, Europeans had been trading partners and not necessarily rivals or enemies, roles more likely to be played by neighbouring African states. Therefore, neighbours of West African slave-trading states were often prepared to help Europeans overcome their traditional enemies, who had long raided them for captives to sell into slavery. Many African states even provided military support for European colonising armies.

Despite trading firearms into Africa for more than a century, Europeans were much better armed. European armies had access to the latest weapons technology, which was developing rapidly in the final decades of the 19th century. Some African armies possessed breech-loading rifles (loaded through the rear of the barrel rather than through the muzzle), but none had the newly-developed machine gun and, with almost the sole exception of Ethiopia, none had artillery with explosive shells. African bravery and strategic skill resulted in a few memorable African victories, such as the Zulu victory over the British in the Battle of Isandlwana in 1879. However, with resources of equipment and soldiers at their disposal, European victory was virtually inevitable. Often it was a very one-sided fight. In 1898 at Omdurman, Sudan, the British killed 20,000 Sudanese fighters in a matter of hours.

Some of the longest struggles for political survival occurred in what was to become French West Africa, where Samory Toure's Mandinka state fought off French incursion from the early 1880s until 1898. Sudanese military leader Rabih al-Zubayr, using a disciplined and well-armed cavalry, waged a Jihad in the Chad region and conquered until 1900, when two French armies converging from north and the south finally overcame Rabih.

In many parts of Africa, rural people were initially unaware of the fact that European powers had, on paper, taken over. Rural resistance to European presence, when it came, was often small in scale but long in duration.

Victory At Adwa

Ethiopia stands as the exception to the rule in the Scramble. Menelik II became emperor in 1889 and proceeded to use the powerful, well-equipped Ethiopian army to expand South, East, and West, incorporating the territories of Oromo, Sidama, and Somali people into his empire. Italy, which had taken Eritrea from the Ottoman Empire in the late 1880s, invaded Ethiopia in 1895, anticipating an easy victory. The Ethiopian army, using breech-loading rifles and artillery, annihilated the Italian force at the Battle of Adwa in 1896. With this victory, Ethiopia became the only indigenous African state to successfully resist European colonisation during the Scramble for African.

Colonial Rule

By World War I (1914 – 1918) Ethiopia and Liberia were the only independent national left in Africa. France and Britain held the most African territory: French colonies stretched across almost all of West Africa, while Britain held an almost unbroken string of colonies from Egypt to South Africa.

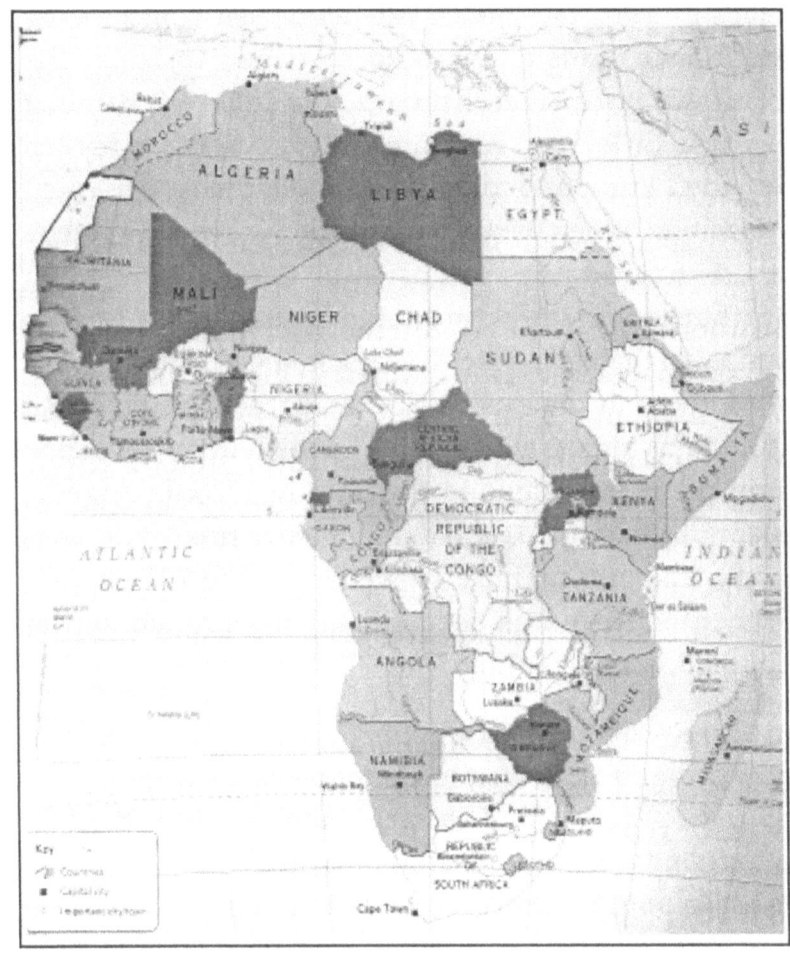

Figure 4.1: Map of Africa

Colonial North Africa

European colonial control came earlier to North Africa than to most of the continent. As the British occupied Egypt in 1882, the French extended their control from Algeria to Tunisia. Morocco managed to resist the establishment of a French protectorate until 1912. Banding together in Islamic resistance forces, North Africans provided European colonists with their most persistent opposition. When the Italians invaded Libya in 1911 they faced formidable opposition from the Sanusi Brotherhood, who conducted a brilliant guerrilla campaign that lasted for 20 years. In the Northern extent of Morocco in the early 1920s the Barbers of the Er Rif Mountains almost expelled the Spanish from the region until the French came to their aid in 1926. In Algeria, Islamic brotherhoods had fought French rule for decades in the mid-19th century. However, by the 20th century French control was secure, and the French settler population rose rapidly.

In early – 20th century Egypt, anti-colonial opposition, protests, and riots were commonplace, as were violent British reactions. The pressure on the British, compounded by the demands of World War I, led Britain to make political concessions. In 1922 Egyptians gained nominal independence and a parliament under King Fuad I, although Britain remained in control behind the scenes. The corruption and ineffectiveness of Fuad's government undermined the parliamentary system as a viable form of government. In the 1930s an organisation called the Muslim Brotherhood emerged in vehement opposition to parliamentary government as well as European culture and interference. This brotherhood inspired other movements throughout Islamic North Africa, and its impact is still felt in the region.

Colonial Sub-Saharan Africa

Across most of sub-Saharan Africa, colonial rule was accompanied by the exploitation of the continent's raw materials by private European concessionary companies. The conduct of these companies was often brutal. The worst excesses were in the Congo (now the Democratic Republic of the Congo), which Belgian king Leopold II ruled as his personal fiefdom until it was taken over by the Belgian government in 1908. Leopold's agents used forced African labour to collect rubber, and regularly tortured and mutilated African workers. Violence by concessionary companies was also experienced in British Southern Rhodesia (now Zimbabwe); German East, West and Southwest Africa (now Tanzania, Cameroon, and Namibia); Portuguese Mozambique; and French Equatorial Africa (now several countries, including Gabon, Republic of the Congo, and Central African Republic).

In the early 20th century European colonists in Africa directed the building of new infrastructures, such as port facilities and numerous railways. Railways were built with African forced labour and the railway companies were often paid with vast grants of African land or mineral concessions. Almost exclusively, the railways linked the source of a colony's agricultural or mineral wealth with ports. They were arteries by which colonising powers extracted the continent's raw materials to benefit themselves, with virtually no thought given to local African economies. Although Europeans would later claim that they had given Africa a modern infrastructure, Africans had paid for it and Europeans were the main beneficiaries. Furthermore, land along the railways became valuable commercial farmland because of the easy access to wider urban or international markets, and so it was often set aside for white settlement. In Kenya, a railway built to link Uganda with the coast provided the British with the incentive to seize the Kikuyu highlands of Kenya for exclusive white settlement.

Colonial taxation of Africans was an important method of control. Throughout much of the continent but especially in countries with extensive white settlement, such as Kenya, Rhodesia (Zimbabwe), and South Africa – taxation was used as a deliberate tool to drive Africans into the labour market. In order to earn the money to pay the new taxes, Africans had to work European farms and mines. Colonists encouraged Africans to migrate from rural areas to work their various enterprises. They recruited men from rural areas and paid them minimal wages on short, fixed – term contracts. Colonists assumed that the workers' wives who remained behind would be able to grow enough food to feed their families' children and elderly. The reality was that rural areas became impoverished by the absence of male labour and insufficient income from wages to compensate. Women therefore often followed men to urban areas in search of casual employment, further impoverishing the rural areas. This migratory pattern would persist throughout the 20th century.

African farmers who were able to retain their land grew a variety of crops for the new colonial markets. They grew groundnuts in the Senegal and Gambia River valleys and in Northern Nigeria. Palm oil continued as an important product of the forest region, from Cote d'Ivoire to the Niger River deltas, while cocoa planting was adopted by the Akan of the Ashanti forest of the Gold Coast (modern Ghana). In Uganda, local African initiative ensured the development of thriving cotton production for export by rail to Indian Ocean ports.

Minor rebellions were widespread in colonial Africa wherever land was seized for white use, forced labour was particularly oppressive, or taxation was harshly or unreasonably imposed. Major rebellions aimed at expelling coloniser altogether erupted in Rhodesia (1896 – 1897), German Southwest Africa (modern-day Namibia, 1904 – 1907) and German East Africa (now Tanzania), however many reinforcements were needed to suppress these rebellions.

Apartheid

In South Africa, Africans suffered the most extreme form of colonisation. The British controlled the entire area following their victory over the independent Boer republics in the South Africa War; or Boer War (1899 – 1902). In 1910 Britain established the Union of South Africa, granting the white population – both British and Afrikaners – control of their own parliamentary government. Between 1910 and 1940 successive white governments pursued increasingly restrictive policies of segregation, which included restricting Africans to Bantustans (homelands) that amounted to a mere 13 percent of the country's land area. For the most part, Africans were only allowed into the white areas, "which included all the cities, if they were employed by whites. What emerged was an unbalanced economic system based upon race, designed for the benefit of whites and dependent on the subservience of blacks. It evolved haphazardly in the first half of the 20th century, but following 1948 the national Party government codified it into the apartheid (Afrikaans for "separateness") system, which lasted until 1994.

Africa And The World Wars

World War I impacted many parts of Africa as British, French, and Belgian forces invaded their neighbouring German colonies. Africans suffered badly, mostly as noncombatant forced labourers. In addition, many thousands served in the French Army as combatants in the trenches of Western Europe. After the war, Germany's African colonies were handed over to neighbouring colonial powers.

World War II (1939 – 1945) combat was limited to Ethiopia and North Africa. Fascist Italy invaded Ethiopia in 1935 and, with the use of aerial bombardment and poison gas, conquered it in 1935. Driven into exile, Ethiopian emperor Haile Selassie failed to gain any wide support for Ethiopia until Italy declared war on Britain in 1940. With the aid of British troops and volunteers from all over Africa, Ethiopians expelled the Italians in 1941 and Hails Selassie was restored to the throne. In North Africa, the British, Germans, and Italians fought a hugely destructive war across the deserts of Libya and Tunisia until 1943. African volunteers from British – and French – controlled areas served in the Allied army in Europe and Asia.

In the long term, the most significant impact of World War II on Africa was political and psychological. The brief colonisation and subsequent liberation of Ethiopia had galvanised the emerging class of urban, educated Africans. These people were determined that the war-fought and won in the name of freedom – should liberate them too. Throughout the continent, from Algeria to Ghana to South Africa, Africans awoke with a new determination to bring an end to the humiliation of colonisation.

The Winning Of Independence

After World War II the dominant African colonial powers, French and Britain, were too economically weakened to resist African demands for political reform. They hoped, however, that even as they loosened their political grip upon the continent, the colonial economic subservience of Africa to Europe could be maintained.

North Africa

In some parts of North Africa, independence came fairly quickly and smoothly after the war: Libya became independent in 1952, and both Morocco and Tunisia in 1956. Meanwhile, in Algeria, the numerous and powerful French colonialists were determined that it would remain part of France. The bitter and bloody Algerian War of Independence was fought until the French finally conceded independence in 1962. In Egypt, radical Muslim army officers overthrew the British puppet government in 1952, led by Gamal Abdel Nasser, they redistributed Egyptian land to the peasantry and nationalised the Suez Canal in 1956. This was the final symbol of Egyptian independence from Europe, and the failure of Britain's attempt to regain the canal signalled to the rest of Africa that the colonial bluff had been called.

French Sub-Saharan Colonies

In sub-Saharan Africa, the French were quickest with political reform. Across French West Africa and French Equatorial Africa, the French allowed the election of local government representatives and in return received African agreement to maintain close economic ties with France. In 1946 the French established a common West African French currency, the CFA franc (franc de la commuaute financiere Africaine, or franc of the African financial community). The currency exchange at a fixed rate with the French franc, assured that virtually all of France's decolonising African territories would continue to bank, invest, and trade with France. All of France's sub-Saharan colonies became independent in 1960, except Guinea (1958) and Djibouti (1977).

British Colonies And South Africa

The British decolonising process was more haphazard and often more African – driven in its initiatives. The Gold Coast led the way, becoming independent Ghana in 1957. Thereafter, the pace of liberation of British colonies largely depended on how long it took the population to agree on its leaders and form of government. Most sub-Saharan British colonies became independent in the period from 1960 to 1964. It was only in the colonies with substantial numbers of white settlers that the process was seriously delayed or fought over. Thus, the Mau Mau rebellion of the 1950s was required to persuade the British to drop their backing of white settler power in Kenya. The British did little to prevent the white settlers of Southern Rhodesia from declaring the independence of their own white minority regime in 1965. After a decade of guerrilla warfare, Zimbabwe was finally liberated in 1980.

White settler power in industrialised South Africa was more entrenched. The white South African government overrode the wave of African nationalism in the 1960s and 1970s by the use of widespread oppression and imprisonment. Through the 1980s internal rebellious pressures combined with the loss of Western support finally prompted the South African – occupied Namibia became independent in 1990, and the government negotiated an end to the oppressive apartheid system with the country's African majority from 1990 to 1994.

Africa Into The 21ST Century

Africa's political inheritance from colonial rule was a mass of artificial "national" with arbitrarily drawn borders and ethnically diverse population with few or no historical ties. In the build-up to independence, "nationalism" presented only a façade of unity in the face of the colonial opponent. After independence, that unity only survived while the new African government was able to deliver on its promise to improve the lives of its citizens, particularly in terms of employment and social services.

The colonial powers had been at pains to emphasise ethnic diversity, as a way to weaken national opposition. They had encouraged a sense of ethnic difference and rivalry far greater than that which had existed in pre-colonial times. In the most extreme version of this policy, for instance, the German and Belgian rulers of Rwanda and Burundi had encouraged Hutu and Tutsi adversity. They co-opted the Tutsi aristocracy as their partners in colonial rule and, in doing so, deprived the Hutu peasantry of educational and economic opportunities. In this policy lay the seeds of Hutu – Tutsi ethnic hatred that was to lead to massacres and genocides in the 1990s. In many democratic nations of independent Africa, political parties developed around ethnic identity. As a result, insecure governments constantly feared ethnic conflict or secession. The fear was well founded, as shown by the 1967 secession of the Igbo homeland, called Biafra, from Nigeria, leading to the Nigerian Civil War (1967 – 1970).

In the 1960s, fear of divisive tendencies encouraged many African governments to set up one party states, in which it was argued that the entire population could work together for the common good of development. In practices, this allowed weak governments to become dictatorial in order to stay in power. In many of these cases, the country's military responded by intervening and sizing power by forces.

In first decades of independence, military intervention was often welcomed by urban population who felt betrayed by weak civilian governments tainted by corruption and failed economic schemes. Military governments proved no better, however, and they too supported themselves by corruption. Many grew even more brutally dictatorial and, unrestricted by constitutional rule, committed atrocities against their perceived opponents. Among the most extreme examples were the rules of Idi Amin of Uganda and Jean – Bedel Bokassa of the Central African Republic, both overthrown in 1979. Through the 1980s many dictators were kept in power by external support, usually in the name of Cold War politics.

It was not until this support was withdrawn around 1990, at the end of the Cold War that most African people had the chance to demand accountability from their governments. From 1990 to 1994 most countries established or re-established military systems of elective government. Citizens voted long – standing autocratic governments out of office in countries such as Nigeria, Mali, Malawi, and Zambia while the more astute military rulers, such as Jerry Rawlings of Ghana, discarded their uniforms and were elected as civilian presidents.

Several African countries went against the trend, ousting dictatorial and military governments in favour of multiparty democracy in the first half of the 1990s. The scale of military corruption in oil – rich Nigeria delayed the process until the late 1990s. Mobotu's 1997 overthrow by armed rebellion created the instability that slid the Congo into outright civil war in the late 1990s and early 21st century. In Algeria, when it appeared that a militant Islamist party was about to win 1992 legislative elections, the Algerian military cancelled the election, suspended the legislature, and ushered in a decade of violent civil conflict. In Libya, the long – standing one-party regime of revolutionary leader Muammar al-Qaddafi ruled on supported by huge oil wealth, reasonably redistributed among a sparse population.

Although a new era of accountability in governance arrived in Africa in the 1990s, it is still very unstable, and military coup d'etat still occurs. Nevertheless – as in the cases of The Gambia, Sierra Leone, and Niger in the mid- or late 1990s – an incoming military ruler now has to justify his presence by declaring that he is only there temporarily to right some specific wrongs and to re-establish civilian democracy within a very short time span. Africans no longer tolerate indefinite dictatorships.

However, the proliferation of weapons across the continent, economic hardship, and weak government infrastructures has combined to encourage banditry and civil conflict across much of Africa. In West Africa, a violent civil war in Liberia in the 1990s spilled over into Sierra Leone, where it continued long after peace returned to Liberia. Even Cote d'Ivoire –long a model of stability – has not been immune from violent conflicts. However, African governments have taken up a collective sense of responsibility and are prepared to intervene on a regional basis to settle disputes or even to restore peace and order.

Africa And The World Economy

Africans are faced with widespread poverty, ill health, and lack of educational opportunities. Despite the positive political developments of the late 20th century, many African governments have been unable to improve their peoples' standards of living. The foundation of Africa's disadvantaged position has been its economic role in the world trading system.

Around the mid-19th Century African economies were increasingly reworked to meet the needs of industrial Europe. Virtually all economic transaction and communication between neighbouring states stopped if they were ruled by different colonial powers. African manufacturing was discouraged, and even banned, if it was likely to compete with the interests of European manufacturers. Indigenous African industry dwindled, and Africa was forced to import virtually all of its manufactured consumer goods. This was the economic system that Africa inherited at independence.

Africa became more dependent and the prices paid for its exported raw materials were set in the major financial markets of the world: New York City, London, Paris, Frankfurt, Hong Kong, and Tokyo. The full implications of this were powerfully demonstrated during the energy crisis of 1973. As oil prices quadrupled, the Western World went into recession and African commodity prices tumbled. Although North African oil producers benefited, sub-Saharan Africans were not yet oil producers on a significant scale and they too suffered from the hike in oil prices. The industrial world paid less and less for African commodities, while at the same time demanded higher and higher prices for its manufactured goods, which Africans needed to import. In this way Africa helped subsidise the industrial world's economic recovery, while most African countries spiralled into debt, poverty, corruption, and political instability, from which they have spent decades trying to recover.

Since the 1980s the industrial world's financial tools, the International Monetary Fund (IMF) and the International Bank for Reconstruction and Development (World Bank), have proposed solutions to Africa's chronic indebtedness. These solutions have been based upon the economics of developed economies, however, rather than upon the specialized needs of developing countries. They have directed African development plans to increased raw material exports, in order to generate the foreign exchange to pay back Africa's debts. But as Africans export more coffee, for example, the price of coffee falls. Thus, Africans work harder and receive less for their efforts. The ultimate goal of the IMF and World Bank has been to enable Africa to pay its debts rather than to enable Africa to develop the self – sufficient ability to compete on equal terms with the industrialised world. They have succeeded in their goal: Africa pays back more in debt servicing than it receives in direct aid. But this means that governments have less to spend on health and education, leading to falling living standards.

African leaders are striving to establish regional trading groups to strengthen their position in the global market. In 2002 they inaugurated the African Union, an organisation intended eventually to establish a common economic market and political union across the entire continent. Achieving this goal, which would make Africa a formidable world power, remains Africa's primary task for the 21st century.

Contributed By: James L. Newman; Assefa Mehretu; Kevin Shillington; Robert Stock.
Microsoft @ Encarta @ 2009. @ 1993 Microsoft Corporation. All rights reserved.

Organisation Of African Unity (OAU)

Background

The creation of the Organisation of African Unity (OAU) by 30 African heads of state and governments, in Addis Ababa on May 25 1963, was the culmination of successive attempts at establishing an inter-African organisation.

Before 1963 many attempts were made to form a continental organisation, but they were thwarted by political, linguistic and economic differences. Among the important early moves were the drafting by Ghana and Guinea on November 23 1958 of a charter (later signed also by Mali) providing for a Union of African States, and the holding of an All – Africa People's Conference in Accra later that year. Earlier in 1958 there was the first conference of Independent African States, also in Accra.

On January 7 1961, representatives of Ghana, Guinea, Mali, Morocco, Libya, Egypt and the Algerian Provisional Government, meeting in Casablanca, adopted a Charter which later became known as the Casablanca Charter. The Charter provided for a joint military command and an African common market. Members of the Casablanca Group advocated the socialist development of all Africa around a strong central authority. Their stand was supported by the newly formed Pan-African Movement for East, Central and Southern Africa (PAFMECSA).

At the invitation of President William Tubman of Liberia, 19 other independent countries opposed to that idea met in Monrovia from May 8 to May 12 1961, and discussed the formation of a new group. The countries were Cameroon, Central African Republic, Chad, Congo (Brazzaville), Dahomey, Ethiopia, Gabon, Ivory Coast, Liberia, Madagascar, Mauritania, Niger, Nigeria, Senegal, Sierra Leone, Somalia, Togo, Tunisia and Upper Volta. The countries, which became known as the Monrovia Group, met again in Lagos in January 1962, and adopted a draft charter for an Organisation of Inter – African and Malagasy States. The Lagos meeting was not attended by Tunisia, which had been present at the Monrovia talks, but Congo (Leopoldville), later Zaire now Congo Democratic Republic which had been absent in Monrovia, attended.

Despite the differences in interests and aims, the ideal of a continental organisation remained, and African leaders continued to strive towards its achievement. On the initiative of Emperor Haile Selassie of Ethiopia moves were started to resolve the differences between the Monrovia and Casablanca groups, culminating in a meeting of foreign ministers of 30 African countries in Addis Ababa in May 1963, to prepare an agenda for a conference of African Heads of State and Government.

Countries represented at the meeting of foreign ministers were Algeria, Burundi, Cameroon, Central African Republic, Congo (Brazzaville), Congo (Leopoldville) now Zaire, Dahomey now Benin, Ethiopia, Gabon, Ghana, Guinea, Cote d'Ivoire, Liberia, Libya, Madagascar, Mali, Mauritania, Morocco, Nigeria, Nigeria, Rwanda, Senegal, Sierra Leone, Somalia, Sudan, Tanganyika now Tanzania, Tunisia, Uganda, Egypt and Upper Volta now Burkina Faso.

The foreign ministers discussed the creation of an organisation of African states, collective defence, decolonization, co-operation among African states in the economic, social, educational, cultural and scientific fields; they also discussed apartheid and racial discrimination, the effects of economic groupings on the development of the continent, disarmament, creation of a permanent conciliation commission, and Africa's role at the United Nations.

The Heads of State conference, which opened in Addis Ababa on May 23 1963 under the chairmanship of Emperor Haile Selassie, approved a Charter establishing the Organisation of African Unity. It was signed by the 30 Heads of States and Government on May 26 1963.

The Charter reflected a compromise between the concept of a loose association of a states favoured by the Monrovia Group and a stronger federation of African states advocated by the Casablanca Group. In proclaiming OAU principles and objectives, the funding members envisaged a unity 'that transcends ethnic and national differences'.

Aims And Objectives

The Charter sets out the following as the aims and objectives of the organisation: to promote the unity and solidarity of the African States; to coordinate and intensify efforts to achieve a better life for the peoples of Africa; to defend their sovereignty, territorial integrity and independence; to eradicate all forms of colonialism from Africa; and to promote international co-operation, having due regard to the Charter of the United Nation and the Universal Declaration of Human Rights.

Member states pledged themselves to harmonise their policies to achieve political and diplomatic co-operation, economic co-operation, including transport and communication, educational and cultural co-operation, health, sanitation and nutritional co-operation, scientific and technical co-operation for defence and security.

The Charter enshrines seven fundamental principles, viz. the sovereign equality of all member States; non-interference in the internal affairs of States; respect for the sovereignty and territorial integrity of each State and for its inalienable right to independent existence; peaceful settlement of disputes by negotiation, mediation, conciliation and arbitration; unreserved condemnation of political assassination in all its forms as well as of subversive activities on the part of neighbouring States or any other State; absolute dedication to the total emancipation of African territories which are still dependent, and nonalignment with regards to all power blocs.

Membership is open to all independent African States and neighbouring islands. The OAU's stand on South Africa has been non-recognition of its regime until majority rule prevails. Liberation movements recognized by the OAU are granted observer status at its meetings.

OAU revenue is derived from contributions by member States, based on their United Nations assessment; funds to aid national liberation movements are provided by member States according to a scale based on national income.

The organisation's headquarters are in Addis Ababa. It also has regional offices in various African capitals, all of them including the Addis Ababa headquarters, employing a staff of 300. The official languages are Arabic, English and French.

Organs Of OAU

The Assembly of Heads of State and Government is the supreme organ and policy-making body of the OAU; it meets annually. There are four standing specialized commissions: the Economic, Social, Transport and Communications Commission, the Defence Commission, the Labour Commission and the Scientific, Cultural, Educational and Health Commission. Ad hoc commissions are set up whenever necessary, especially for peacemaking efforts.

The OAU was later transformed to become African Union, patterned on the basis of the European Union, with a parliament Commission and other structures which aim at bringing African countries together.

In addition to O.A.U (now A.U) there are sub-regional organisations which include the following:-

- a) The Economic Community of West African States (ECOWAS);

- b) The Customs and Economic Union of Central Africa (UDEAC);

- c) The Southern African Development Coordination Conference (SADCC):

There are also Pan – African organisations such as Economic Commission for Africa (ECA), the African Development Bank (ADB), the Organisation of African Trade Union Unity (OATUU), etc.

Table 4.1: Population of Countries in Africa

Population Of African Countries As At 2006

World Total	-	6,602,237,000
Africa	-	934,500,000
1. Algeria	-	33,333,000
2. Angola	-	12,263,000
3. Benin	-	8,078,000
4. Botswana	-	1,816,000
5. Burundi	-	8,391,000
6. Burkina Faso	-	14,326,000
7. Cameroon	-	18,060,000
8. Cape Verde	-	424,000
9. Chad	-	9,886,000
10. Central African Republic	-	4,369,000
11. Comoros	-	711,000
12. Congo Dem Rep. of	-	65,752,000
13. Cote d'Ivoire	-	18,013,000
14. Djibouti	-	496,000

15.	Egypt -	80,335,000
16.	Equatorial Guinea -	551,000
17.	Eritrea -	4,907,000
18.	Ethiopia -	76,512,000
19.	Gabon -	1,455,000
20.	Gambia, The -	1,678,000
21.	Ghana -	22,931,000
22.	Guinea -	9,947,000
23.	Guinea Bissau -	1,473,000
24.	Kenya -	36,914,000
25.	Lesotho -	2,125,000
26.	Liberia -	3,196,000
27.	Libya -	6,037,000
28.	Madagascar -	19,449,000
29.	Malawi -	13,603,000
30.	Mali -	11,995,000
31.	Mauritania -	3,270,000
32.	Mauritius -	1,251,000
33.	Mayotte -	209,000
34.	Morocco -	33,757,000
35.	Mozambique -	20,906,000

36.	Namibia	2,055,000
37.	Niger	12,895,000
38.	Nigeria	140,431,000
39.	Rwanda	9,908,000
40.	Sahara Western	383,000
41.	Saint Helena	8,000
42.	Sao Tome and Principe	200,000
43.	Senegal	12,522,000
44.	Seychelles	82,000
45.	Sierra Leone	6,145,000
46.	Somalia	9,119,000
47.	South Africa	43,998,000
48.	Sudan	39,380,000
49.	Swaziland	1,133,000
50.	Tanzania	39,384,000
51.	Togo	5,702,000
52.	Tunisia	10,276,000
53.	Uganda	30,263,000
54.	Zambia	11,477,000
55.	Zimbabwe	12,311,000

Source: The Economist Diary 2009
* Final Result, Nigerian Population Census 2006.

Chapter 5

Know The World

Ancient Rome: Introduction

Ancient Rome, the period between the 8th and 1st centuries BC in which Rome grew from a tiny settlement to an emerging empire while developing from monarchy to a republican form of government.

Nearly 3,000 years ago shepherds first built huts on the hills beside the Tiber River in central Italy. These encampments gradually grew and merged to form the city of Rome. Rome's history is unique in comparison to other large urban centres like London, England, or Paris, France, because it encompasses more than the story of a single city. In ancient times Rome extended its political control over all of Italy and eventually created an empire that stretched from England to North Africa and from the Atlantic Ocean to Arabia. The political history of Rome is marked by three periods. In the first period from 753-509 BC, the city developed from a village to a city ruled by kings. Then, the Romans expelled the kings and established the Roman Republic during the period from 509-27 BC. Following the collapse of the republic, Rome fell under the domination of emperors and flourished for another five centuries as the Roman Empire from 27 BC-AD 476.

The Romans also had enormous cultural influence. Their language, Latin, gave rise to languages spoken by a billion people in the world today. Many other languages—including Polish, Turkish, and Vietnamese—use the Roman alphabet. The Romans developed a legal system that remains the basis of continental European law, and they brought to portraiture a lifelike style that forms the basis of the realistic tradition in Western art. The founders of the American government looked to the Roman Republic as a model. Modern political institutions also reflect Roman origins: senators, bicameral legislatures, judges, and juries are all adapted from the Roman system. In addition, despite recent modernization, the Roman Catholic Church still uses symbols and ritual derived largely from the ancient Romans.

Middle Ages

Introduction

Middle Ages, period in the history of Europe that lasted from about AD 350 to about 1450. At the beginning of the Middle Ages, the western half of the Roman Empire began to fragment into smaller, weaker kingdoms. By the end of the Middle Ages, many modern European states had taken shape. During this time, the precursors of many modern institutions, such as universities and bodies of representative government, were created.

Heirs Of The Roman Empire: Byzantium, Islam, and the West

By 750 the Roman world had given way to three heirs: the Byzantine Empire, Islam, and the West. All three had much in common. The most fundamental of these similarities was religion. The people in all three areas believed in one God, and they also agreed that spiritual and worldly things were bound together—that is, they did not believe in the separation of church and state. Another similarity involved the rural orientation of Byzantium, Islam, and the West. In all three regions, farming was the most important and most common occupation of the inhabitants. A third similarity had to do with loyalties. In all three worlds, people's relationships were local in nature. They cared more about neighbours and local leaders than about the rulers at the top, who were often too far away to make their presence felt. This led to tensions between central and local authorities, with important political results: Large states tended to fragment into smaller ones, some of which proved very resilient and have lasted until modern times.

The Byzantine Empire, the Islamic world, and the West also had many differences. The most important of these were economic and political. On the whole, the Islamic world was prosperous, with thriving trade and a large merchant and professional class. Byzantium came next. Although the Byzantine economy was hurt by war and loss of territory, it quickly revived, Constantinople remained an important centre of trade, and the Byzantine countryside was productive. The imperial administration was able to collect taxes from peasants without difficulty. The West was the poorest heir of the

Roman Empire. While a very wealthy land — owning class lived well, many cities of the West were depopulated and the land was relatively unproductive.

Another difference among the heirs of the Roman Empire was political. The Byzantine Empire was a centralized state, with the emperor acting as an important figure in both spiritual and worldly matters. The emperor appointed the patriarch of Constantinople—the head of the church—and called councils to consider matters of church law and policy. At the same time, the emperor was head of the army and navy and often personally led troops into battle. A well-organised civil service worked for him, keeping records and collecting taxes.

In the Islamic world, the caliphs were also strong, centralized rulers. Like the Byzantine emperors, the caliphs had a well-organized civil service and efficient methods of collecting taxes. This centralisation reached its height at the end of the 8th century under Harun ar-Rashid, who was one of the most powerful of the caliphs. From his capital city at Baghdad (today the capital of Iraq), he ruled over lands that stretched more than 5,800 km (3,600 mi) from east to west—about 1,600 km (1,000 mi) longer than the length of the United States. He was a successful military leader and a patron of the arts, and he was enormously wealthy.

In contrast with these realms, the West was fragmented, with little or no governmental centralization. For example, what would later become England was divided into many small kingdoms. The Italian peninsula was divided among a king in the north, dukes in the south, and Byzantine governors in between. In addition, the pope (the bishop of Rome, theoretically under the rule of the Byzantine emperor) thought he ought to have his own Italian territories to rule. In what would become France and Germany, a royal family called the Merovingians ruled over several kingdoms and often fought among themselves.

If one observed all the regions of the former Roman Empire in about the year 800, one might predict that West would become a backwater, while the Islamic world and the Byzantine empire would become superpowers. This prediction would be entirely wrong in regard to the Byzantine Empire: By the end of the Middle Ages it had disappeared entirely. It would be half –right about the Islamic world, which continued to be strong and remains so today, although the Muslims became disunited politically and even religiously. The most astonishing outcome was the fate of the West, which became Europe. By the end of the Middle Ages, Europe was organized into strong, prosperous, competitive, and aggressive states, and European explorers and traders were launching expeditions to China, Africa, and eventually the Americas.

Origins Of The Crusades

After the death of Charlemagne, king of the Franks, in 814 and the subsequent collapse of his empire, Christian Europe was under attack and on the defensive. Magyars, nomadic people from Asia, pillaged eastern and central Europe until the 10th century. Beginning about 800, several centuries of Viking raids disrupted life in northern Europe and even threatened Mediterranean cities. But the greatest threat came from the forces of Islam, militant and victorious in the centuries following the death of their leader, Muhammad, in 632. By the 8th century, Islamic forces had conquered North Africa, the eastern shores of the Mediterranean, and most of Spain. Islamic armies established bases in Italy, greatly reduced the size and power of the Byzantine Empire (the Eastern Roman Empire) and besieged its capital, Constantinople. The Byzantine Empire, which had preserved much of the classical civilization of the Greeks and had defended the eastern Mediterranean from assaults from all sides, was barely able to hold off the enemy. Islam posed the threat of a rival culture and religion, which neither the Vikings nor the Magyars had done.

In the 11th century the balance of power began to swing toward the West. The church became more centralized and stronger from a reform movement to end the practice whereby kings installed important clergy, such as bishops, in office. Thus, For the first time in many years, the popes were able to effectively unite European popular support behind them, a factor that contributed greatly to the popular appeal of the first crusades.

Furthermore, Europe's population was growing, its urban life was beginning to revive, and both long distance and local trade were gradually increasing. European human and economic resources could now support new enterprises on the scale of the Crusades. A growing population and more surplus wealth also meant greater demand for goods from elsewhere. European traders had always looked to the Mediterranean; now they sought greater control of the goods, routes, and profits.

Thus worldly interests coincided with religious feelings about the Holy Land and the pope's newfound ability to mobilize and focus a great enterprise.

First Crusade

It was against this background that Pope Urban II, in a speech at Clermont in France in November 1095, called for a great Christian expedition to free Jerusalem from the Seljuk Turks, a new Muslim power that had recently begun actively harassing peaceful Christian pilgrims travelling to Jerusalem. The pope was spurred by his position as the spiritual head of Western Europe, by the temporary absence of strong rulers in Germany (the Holy Roman Empire) or France who could either oppose or take over the effort, and by a call for help from the Byzantine emperor, Alexius 1. These various factors were genuine causes, and at the same time, useful justifications for the pope's call for a Crusade. In any case, Urban's speech-well reported in several chronicles-appealed to thousands of people of all classes. It was the right message at the right time.

The First Crusade, which began in 1096, was successful in its explicit aim of freeing Jerusalem. It also established a Western Christian military presence in the Near East that lasted for almost 200 years. The Crusaders called this area *Outremer*, French for "beyond the seas." The First Crusade was the wonder of its day. It attracted no European kings and few major nobles, drawing mainly lesser barons and their followers. They came primarily from the lands of French culture and language, which is why Westerners in Outremer were referred to as Franks.

To the rulers of Muslim states a concerted military effort was imperative. The Franks were an affront to religious as well as to political and economic interests. The combination of zeal and luck that had enabled the Crusaders to triumph in 1099 evaporated in the face of such realities as the need to recruit and maintain soldiers who were loyal and effective. Islamic rulers turned almost at once to the offensive, though a major blow to Christian power did not come until 1144, when the Muslims recaptured Edessa. The city of Edessa had guarded the back door of the Frankish holdings, which were mostly near the coast. This loss marked the beginning of the end of a viable Christian military bastion against Islam.

News of the fall of Edessa reverberated throughout Europe, and the Second Crusade was called by Pope Eugenius III. Though the enthusiasm of 1095 was never again matched, a number of major figures joined the Second Crusade, including Holy Roman Emperor Conrad III and France's King Louis VII. Conrad made the mistake of choosing the land route from Constantinople to the Holy Land and his army was decimated at Dorylaeum in Asia Minor. The French army was more fortunate, but it also suffered serious casualties during the journey, and only part of the original force reached Jerusalem in 1148. In consultation with King Baldwin III of Jerusalem and his nobles, the Crusaders decided to attack Damascus in July.

The expedition failed to take the city, and shortly after the collapse of this attack, the French king and the remains of his army returned home. The Second Crusade resulted in many Western casualties· and no gains of value in Outremer. In fact the only military gains during this period were made in what is now Portugal, where English troops, which had turned aside from the Second Crusade, helped free the city of Lisbon from the Moors.

In the years between the failure of the Second Crusade and 1170, when the Muslim prince Saladin came to power In Egypt, the Latin States were on the defensive but were able to maintain themselves. But in 1187 Saladin inflicted a major defeat on a combined army at Hattin and subsequently took Jerusalem. The situation had become dire. In response to the Church's call for a new, major Crusade, three Western rulers undertook to lead their forces in person. These were Richard I, the Lion-Hearted of England, Philip II of France, and Frederick I, called Frederick Barbarossa, the Holy Roman Emperor. Known as the Third Crusade, it has become perhaps the most famous of all Crusades other than the First Crusade, though its role in legend and literature greatly outweighs its success or value.

The three rulers were rivals. Richard and Philip had long been in conflict over the English holdings in France. Though English kings had inherited great fiefs in France, their homage to the French king was a constant source of trouble. Frederick Barbarossa, old and famous, died in 1189 on the way to the Holy Land, and most of his armies returned to Germany following his death. Philip II had been spurred into taking up the Crusade by a need to match his rivals, and he returned home in 1191 with little concern for Eastern glories. But Richard, a great soldier, was very much in his element. He saw an opportunity to campaign in the field, to establish links with the local nobility, and to speak as the voice of the Crusader states. Though he gained much glory, the Crusaders were unable to recapture Jerusalem or much of the former territory of the Latin Kingdom. They did succeed, however, in wresting from Saladin control of a chain of cities along the Mediterranean coast. By October 1192, when Richard finally left the Holy Land, the Latin Kingdom had been reconstituted. Smaller than the original kingdom and considerably weaker militarily and economically, the second kingdom lasted precariously for another century.

Crusades Of The 13th Century

After the disappointments of the Third Crusade, Western forces would never again threaten the real bases of Muslim power. From that point on, they were only able to gain access to Jerusalem through diplomacy, not arms.

In 1199 Innocent III called for another Crusade to recapture Jerusalem. In preparation for this Crusade, the ruler of Venice agreed to transport French and Flemish Crusaders to the Holy Land. However, the Crusaders never fought the Muslims. Unable to pay the Venetians the amount agreed upon, they were forced to bargain with the Venetians. They agreed to take part in an attack on one of the Venetians' rivals, Zara, a trading port on the Adriatic Sea, in the nearby Kingdom of Hungary. When Innocent III learned of the expedition, he excommunicated the participants, but the combined force captured Zara in 1202. The Venetians then persuaded the Crusaders to attack the Byzantine capital of Constantinople, which fell on April 13, 1204. For three days the Crusaders sacked the city. Subsequently the Venetians gained a monopoly on Byzantine trade. The Latin Empire of Constantinople was established, which lasted until the recapture of

Constantinople by the Byzantine emperor in 1261. In addition, several new Crusader states sprang up in Greece and along the Black Sea.

The Fourth Crusade did not even threaten the Muslim powers. Trade and commerce had triumphed, as Venice had hoped, but at the cost of irreparably widening the rift between the Eastern and Western churches. Crusades after the Fourth were not mass movements. They were military enterprises led by rulers moved by personal motives. Holy Roman Emperor Frederick II vowed to lead a Crusade in 1215, but for domestic political reasons postponed his departure. Under pressure from Pope Gregory IX, Frederick and his army finally sailed from Italy in August 1227, but returned to port within a few days because Frederick had fallen ill. The pope, outraged at this further delay, promptly excommunicated the emperor. Undaunted, Frederick embarked for the Holy Land in June 1228. There he conducted his unconventional Crusade almost entirely by diplomatic negotiations with the Egyptian sultan. These negotiations produced a peace treaty by which the Egyptians restored Jerusalem to the Crusaders and guaranteed a ten-year respite from hostilities. However, Frederick was ridiculed in Europe for using diplomacy rather than the sword.

In 1248 Louis IX, Saint Louis of France, decided that his obligations as a son of the Church outweighed those of his throne, and he left his kingdom for a six-year adventure. Since the base of Muslim power had shifted to Egypt, Louis did not even march on the Holy Land; any war against Islam now fit the definition of a Crusade. Louis and his followers landed in Egypt on June 5, 1249, and the following day captured Damietta. The next phase of their campaign, an attack on Cairo in the spring of 1250, proved to be a catastrophe. The Crusaders failed to

guard their flanks, and as a result the Egyptians retained control over the water reservoirs along the Nile. By opening the sluice gates, they created floods that trapped the whole Crusading army, and Louis was forced to surrender in April 1250. After paying an enormous ransom and surrendering Damletta, Louis sailed to Palestine, where he spent four years building fortifications and strengthening the defences of the Latin Kingdom. In the spring of 1254 he and his army returned to France.

King Louis also organised the last major Crusade, in 1270. This time the response of the French nobility was unenthusiastic, and the expedition was directed against the city of Tunis rather than Egypt. It ended abruptly when Louis died in Tunisia during the summer of 1270.

The tale of the Crusader states, after the mid-13th century, is a sad and short one. Though popes, some zealous princes-including Edward I of England-and various religious and political thinkers continued to call for a Crusade to unite the warring armies of Europe and to deliver a smashing blow to Islam, later efforts were too small and too sporadic to do more than buy time for the Crusader states. With the fall of 'Akko (Acre) in 1291, the last stronghold on the mainland was lost, though the military religious orders kept garrisons on Cyprus and Rhodes for some centuries. However, the Crusading impulse was not dead. As late as 1396 a large expedition against the Ottoman Turks in the Balkans, summoned by Siqisrnund of Hungary, drew knights from all over the West. But a crushing defeat at Nicopolis (Nikopol) on the Danube River also showed that the appeal of these ventures far outstripped the political and military support needed for their success.

Consequences and Conclusion

When Judged by narrow military standards, the Crusades were a failure. What was gained so quickly was slowly but steadily lost. On the other hand, to hold territory under a Christian banner so far from home, given the contemporary conditions of transport and communication, was Impressive. The taking of Constantinople during the Fourth Crusade had been just short of fatal to the Byzantine Empire, and it cast a blemish on the movement in the West, where there were critics of the whole concept of armed Crusades. While Constantinople was not taken by the Ottoman Empire until 1453, the Byzantine Empire after the Fourth Crusade was but a shell of its former self.

British Empire

Introduction

British Empire, name given to United Kingdom of Great Britain and Northern Ireland and the former dominions, colonies, and other territories throughout the world that owed allegiance to the British Crown from the late 1500s to the middle of the 20th century. At its height in the early 1900s, the British Empire included over 20 percent of the world's land area and more than 400 million people.

The foundations of the British Empire were laid during the reign of Queen Elizabeth I (1558-1603). Under Elizabeth, English support for naval exploration increased dramatically, and in 1580 Sir Francis Drake became the first Englishman to sail around the world. Overseas commercial and trade interests were also established in the form of the English East India Company in 1600. However, because England was at war with Spain, which had a large colonial empire In the Americas, English colonization in the Americas remained almost unknown in the 16th century. The first real venture was the attempted settlement of Roanoke Island off the North American coast in 1585 by Sir Walter Raleigh. This settlement did not survive, and the English did not attempt further exploration and colonization in the Americas until 1604, after peace had been made with Spain.

The First British Empire

In the 17th and 18th centuries, Britain established its first empire, which was centred in the Caribbean and in North America. It began with the establishment of tobacco plantations in the West Indies and religious colonies along the Atlantic coast of North America. England established a presence in India during the 17th century with the activities of the East India Company. Although this presence became larger and more entrenched during the 17th and 18th centuries, India did not come under direct British rule until 1858.

The American Revolution

For the British, an expanded empire meant new responsibilities and new costs. The British government wanted to tap American revenues to pay for American necessities, and consequently increased taxation with the Stamp Act (1765). Although the British considered the act to be perfectly fair, many American colonists saw it as a violation of their rights. After riots in the colonies, the Stamp Act was repealed, but other taxes soon replaced it, setting off a controversy in which the colonies united against Britain in the Continental Congress. A skirmish at Concord, Massachusetts, in April 1775 deteriorated into general fighting, and in July 1776 the Congress issued the Declaration of Independence. During the American Revolution that followed, the Congress controlled most of the land area, but the British were secure in their stronghold in New York until their position was weakened by a defeat at Saratoga (1777), which encouraged France to intervene on behalf of the rebellious colonists. British resistance ended when General Charles Cornwallis surrendered with his army at Yorktown, Virginia, in October 1781.

This defeat marked not only the end of the American war, but also the end of the First British Empire. Yet because France had not been able to challenge British supremacy at sea, Britain's losses did not extend beyond the American colonies themselves. At the same time, the British presence in Canada was reinforced by the establishment of the colony of New Brunswick, resulting from the migration northwards of over 30,000 citizens of the American colonies who were still loyal to Britain.

The Second British Empire

After the loss of the American colonies, British commerce turned from the Americas to the East in its search both for spices for re-export and, increasingly, for markets to sell ever-growing amounts of British manufactured goods. The Industrial Revolution had transformed the British economy from a primarily agricultural one to one based much more on mechanized manufacturing, and as a result had drastically increased the amount of British products available for export. The quest for new markets for international trade was the economic incentive behind the Second British Empire. Free trade, the belief that international trade should not be restricted by any one nation, replaced the old colonial system, which had relied on mercantilist ideas of protected commerce.

The Second British Empire, focused more on Asia and Africa, continued to expand in the 1800s and early 1900s and reached its apex at the end of World War I. However, a growing nationalism among the British colonies gradually weakened the power of the empire, and Britain was eventually forced to grant independence to many of its former colonies.

Colonialism And Colonies

Introduction

Colonialism and Colonies, one country's domination of another country or people—usually achieved through aggressive, often military, actions—and the territory acquired in this manner. The terms *colonialism* and *imperialism* are sometimes used interchangeably, but scholars usually distinguish between the two, reserving *colonialism* for instances where one country assumes political control over another and using *imperialism* more broadly to refer to political or economic control exercised either formally or informally.

Types Of Colonies

In the past 500 years, there have been several types of colonies. The main ones were colonies of settlement, colonies of exploitation, and what might be called contested settlement colonies. Most European powers established more than one type of colony. The British Empire, for instance, included colonies of settlement (Virginia, Massachusetts, New Zealand, New South Wales), colonies of exploitation (Nigeria, Jamaica, Malaya), a preexisting empire (India), contested settlement colonies (Kenya), and spheres of influence (Argentina). The French Empire also included settlement colonies (Algeria, Quebec), exploitation colonies (Martinique, the French Congo), and a preexisting empire (Indochina).

World War I

Introduction

World War I, military conflict, from August 1914 to November 1918, that involved many of the countries of Europe as well as the United States and other nations throughout the world. .World War I was one of the most violent and destructive wars in European history. Of the 65 million men who were mobilised, more than 10 million were killed and more than 20 million wounded. The term *World War I* did not come into general use until a second worldwide conflict broke out in 1939. Before that year, the war was known as the Great War or the World War.

World War I was the first total war. Once the war began, the countries involved mobilised their entire papulation and economic resources to achieve victory on the battlefield. The term *home front*, which was widely employed for the first time during World War I, perfectly symbolised this new concept of a war in which the civilian population behind the lines was directly and critically involved in the war effort.

The war began as a clash between two coalitions of European countries. The first coalition, known as the Allied Powers, included the United Kingdom, France, Belgium, Serbia, Montenegro, and the Russian Empire . The Central Powers, which opposed them, consisted of the empires of Germany and Austria-Hungary. Japan joined the Allied Powers in 1914. The Ottoman Empire joined the Central Powers in 1914, as did Bulgaria in 1915. The same year, Italy entered the war on the Allied side. Although the United States initially remained neutral, it joined the Allies in 1917. The conflict eventually involved

32 countries, 28 of which supported the Allies. Some of these nations, however, did not participate in the actual fighting.

The immediate cause of the war was the assassination of Archduke Francis Ferdinand, the heir to the throne of Austria-Hungary, by a Serbian nationalist. The fundamental causes of the war however, were rooted deeply in the European history of the previous century particularly in the political and economic policies that prevailed in Europe after 1871, the year that Germany emerged as a major European power.

By the end of 1914, the war entered a stalemate. Both sides became mired in two main, stationary fronts—the western front, primarily in northeastern France, and the eastern front, mainly in western Russia. At the fronts, the troops fought each other from numerous parallel lines of interconnected trenches. Each side laid siege to the other's system of trenches and endeavoured to break through their lines.

When the war finally came to an end on November 11, 1918, and the Central Powers were defeated, the political order of Europe had been transformed beyond recognition. The German, Austro-Hungarian, Russian, and Ottoman empires had collapsed. New areas were carved out of their former lands, and the boundaries of many other countries were redrawn. The war also helped precipitate the Bolshevik Revolution in Russia which ushered in the ideology of Communism there.

The war also had important: long-term consequences. The enormous cost of the war undermined the financial stability of all of the countries involved, and they had to bear an onerous burden of debt for many years to come. These financial losses, combined with the battlefield deaths and physical destruction, severely weakened the European powers.

End Of Hostilities

On November 11, 1918, at 5:00 AM the Allied and German delegates signed an armistice on terms established by the Allies; at 11:00 the same morning, hostilities on the western front came to an end. The end of the war on the 11th hour of the 11th day of the 11th month of 1918 prompted relief and jubilation in all of the belligerent countries. The murderous struggle that had dragged on for over four years had finally ended. Political leaders then took up the task of trying to transform the military armistice into a durable peace.

Aftermath Of World War I

In the aftermath of World War I, the political order of Europe came crashing to the ground. The German, Austro-Hungarian, and Russian empires ceased to exist, and the Ottoman Empire soon followed them into oblivion. New nations emerged, borders were radically shifted, and ethnic conflicts erupted. Victors and vanquished alike faced an enormous recovery challenge after four years of financial loss, economic deprivation, and material destruction. Amid this chaotic situation, the leaders of the victorious coalition assembled in Paris to forge a new international system that would replace the old order. The decisions they made would determine the future of Europe, and much of the rest of the world, for decades to come.

Treaty Of Versailles

Delegates from all of the Allied countries met in Paris, France, in January 1919 to draft the peace treaties. But it soon became evident that real decision-making authority rested in the hands of the leaders of the four states whose economic and military might had defeated the Central Powers: Prime Minister David Lloyd George of Britain, Prime Minister Vittorio Orlando of Italy, Premier Georges Clemenceau of France, and President Woodrow Wilson of the United States. The Japanese delegation was on the same level as the four European powers, but it participated in the conference debates only when matters pertaining to East Asia were discussed.

Britain's principal goal at the peace conference was to remove the threat of German naval power and to end Germany's overseas empire. Once Lloyd George had achieved these two objectives, he pursued a moderate territorial settlement out of concern that a harsh peace would prompt a defeated Germany to try to destroy the new international order. Orlando Wanted the territory that the Allies had promised Italy when it entered the war as well as additional territory on the Adriatic Coast inhabited by Italians. Clemenceau had two principal goals; To establish a set of ironclad guarantees against a future German military threat to France and to require Germany to pay to repair the extensive damage that it had caused to Northeastern France during the war. The United States had no financial or territorial claims against Germany, but President Wilson fought for what he regarded as a peace of justice. He wanted a new international organization known as the League of Nations to be created to help prevent future armed conflicts.

The Treaty of Versailles that the representatives of the new German Republic were compelled to sign on June 28, 1919, was a compromise. On the one hand, Germany was deprived of portions of its prewar territory, such as Alsace and Lorraine, the city of Danzig (Gdansk), and the Polish Corridor. Also Germany was unilaterally disarmed and forced to accept an Allied military occupation of the Rhineland and to give up its colonial empire. Germany was forced to accept responsibility for the outbreak of the war and was required to pay the cost of repairing the wartime damage, known as reparations. On the other hand, Germany emerged from the peace conference as a potentially powerful country because its industrial areas were left intact and it did not lose any vital territory.

The U.S. Senate refused to approve the treaty in part because of internal U.S. politics, and the United States concluded a separate peace treaty with Germany in 1921. Without U.S. support, the economically weakened, war-weary countries of France and Britain were left with the difficult task of enforcing the provisions of the Versailles peace.

World War II

Introduction

World War II, global military conflict that, in terms of lives lost and material destruction, was the most devastating war in human history. It began in 1939 as a European conflict between Germany and an Anglo-French coalition but eventually widened to include most of the nations of the world. It ended in 1945, leaving a new world order dominated by the United States and the Union of

Soviet Socialist Republics (USSR).

More than any previous war, World War II involved the commitment of nations' entire human and economic resources, the blurring of the distinction between combatant and noncombatant, and the expansion of the battlefield to include all of the enemy's territory. The most important determinants of its outcome were industrial capacity and personnel. In the last stages of the war, two radically new weapons were introduced: the long-range rocket and the atomic bomb. In the main, however, the war was fought with the same or improved weapons of the types used in World War I (1914-1918). The greatest advances were in aircraft and tanks.

The World After World War I

Three major powers had been dissatisfied with the outcome of World War I. Germany, the principal defeated nation, bitterly resented the territorial losses and reparations payments imposed on it by the Treaty of Versailles. Italy, one of the victors, found its territorial gains far from enough either to offset the cost of the war or to satisfy its ambitions. Japan, also a victor, was unhappy about its failure to gain control of China.

Causes Of The War

France, the United Kingdom, and the United States had attained their wartime objectives. They had reduced Germany to a military cipher and had reorganized Europe and the world as they saw fit. The French and the British frequently disagreed on policy in the postwar period, however, and were unsure of their ability to defend the peace settlement. The United States, disillusioned by the Europeans' failure to repay their war debts, retreated into isolationism.

The Failure Of Peace Efforts

During the 1920s, attempts were made to achieve a stable peace. The first was the establishment (1920) of the League of Nations as a forum in which nations could settle their disputes. The league's powers were limited to persuasion and various levels of moral and economic sanctions that the members were free to carry out as they saw fit. At the Washington Conference of 1921-22, the principal naval powers agreed to limit their navies according to a fixed ratio. The Locarno Conference (1925) produced a treaty guarantee of the German-French boundary and an arbitration agreement between Germany and Poland. In the Paris Peace Pact (1928), 63 countries, including all the great powers except the USSR, renounced war as an instrument of national policy and pledged to resolve all disputes among them "by pacific means." The signatories had agreed beforehand to exempt wars of "self-defence."

The Rise Of Fascism

One of the victors' stated aims in World War I had been "to make the world safe for democracy," and postwar Germany adopted a democratic constitution, as did most of the other states restored or created after the war. In the 1920s, however, the wave of the future appeared to be a form of nationalistic, militaristic totalitarianism known by its Italian name, fascism. It promised to minister to peoples' wants more effectively than democracy and presented itself as the one sure defence against communism. Benito Mussolini established the first Fascist dictatorship in Italy in 1922.

Formation Of The Axis Coalition

Adolf Hitler, the *Fuhrer* ("leader") of the German National Socialist (Nazi) Party, preached a racist brand of fascism. Hitler promised to overturn the Versailles Treaty and secure additional *Lebensraum* ("living space") for the German people, who he contended deserved more as members of a superior race. In the early 1930s, the depression hit Germany. The moderate parties could not agree on what to do about it, and large numbers of voters turned to the Nazis and Communists. In 1933 Hitler became the German chancellor, and in a series of subsequent moves established himself as dictator.

Japan did not formally adopt fascism, hut the armed forces' powerful position in the government enabled them to impose a similar type of totalitarianism. As dismantlers of the world status quo, the Japanese military were well ahead of Hitler. They used a minor clash with Chinese troops near Mukden in 1931 as a pretext for taking over all of Manchuria, where they proclaimed the puppet state of Manchukuo in 1932. In 1937-1938 they occupied the main Chinese ports.

Having denounced the disarmament clauses of the Versailles Treaty, created a new air force, and reintroduced conscription, Hitler tried out his new weapons on the side of right-wing' military rebels in the Spanish Civil War (1936-1939). The venture brought him into collaboration with Mussolini, who was also supporting the Spanish revolt after having seized (1935-1936) Ethiopia in a small war. Treaties between Germany, Italy, and Japan in the period from 1936 to 1940 brought into being the Rome-Berlin-Tokyo Axis. The Axis thereafter became the collective term for those countries and their allies.

The Defeat Of France

On May 20 the panzer group took Abbeville at the mouth of the Somme River and began to push north along the coast; it covered 400 km (250 mi) in 11 days. By May 26, the British and French were pushed into a narrow beachhead around Dunkerque. The Belgian king, Leopold III, surrendered his army the next day. Destroyers and smaller craft of all kinds rescued 338,226 men from Dunkerque in a heroic sea lift that probably would not have succeeded if the German commander, General Gerd von Rundstedt, had not stopped the tanks to save them for the next phase. On June 5 the Germans launched a new assault against France. Italy declared war on France and Britain on June 10. The Maginot line, which only extended to the Belgian border, was intact, but the French commander, General Maxime Weygand, had nothing with which to screen it or Paris on the north and west. On June 17, Marshal Henri Philippe Petain, a World War I hero who had become premier the day before, asked for an armistice. The armistice was signed on June 25 on terms that gave Germany control of northern France and the Atlantic coast. Petain then set up a capital at Vichy in the unoccupied southeast.

The Battle of Britain

In the summer of 1940, Hitler dominated Europe from the North Cape to the Pyrenees. His one remaining active enemy—Britain, under a new prime minister, Winston Churchill—vowed to continue fighting. Whether it could was questionable. The British army had left most of its weapons on the beaches at Dunkerque. Stalin was in no mood to challenge Hitler. The United States, shocked by the fall of France, began the first peacetime conscription in its history and greatly increased its military budget, but public opinion, although sympathetic to Britain, was against getting into the war.

The Germans hoped to subdue the British by starving them out. In June 1940 they undertook the Battle of the Atlantic, using submarine warfare to cut the British overseas lifelines. The Germans now had submarine bases in Norway and France. At the outset the Germans had only 28 submarines, but more were being built—enough to keep Britain in danger until the spring of 1943 and to carry on the battle for months thereafter.

Invasion was the expeditious way to finish off Britain, but that meant crossing the English Channel; Hitler would not risk it unless the Britain's Royal Air Force could be neutralized first. As a result, the Battle of Britain was fought in the air, not on the beaches. In August 1940 the Germans launched daylight raids against ports and airfields and in September against inland cities. The objective was to draw out the British fighters and destroy them. The Germans failed to reckon with a new device, radar, which greatly increased the British fighters' effectiveness. Because their own losses were too high, the Germans had to switch to night bombing at the end of September. Between then and May 1941 they made 71 major raids on London and 56 on other cities, but the damage they wrought was too indiscriminate to be militarily decisive. On September 17, 1940, Hitler postponed the invasion indefinitely, thereby conceding defeat in the Battle of Britain.

The Beginning Of The War In The Pacific

The seeming imminence of a Soviet defeat in the summer and fall of 1941 had created dilemmas for Japan and the United States. The Japanese thought they then had the best opportunity to seize the petroleum and other resources of Southeast Asia and the adjacent islands; on the other hand, they knew they could not win the war with the United States that would probably ensue. The U.S. government wanted to stop Japanese expansion but doubted whether the American people would be willing to go to war to do so. Moreover, the United States did not want to get embroiled in a war with Japan while it faced the ghastly possibility of being alone in the world with a triumphant Germany. After the oil embargo, the Japanese, also under the pressure of time, resolved to move in Southeast Asia and the nearby islands.

Pearl Harbor

Until December 1941 the Japanese leadership pursued two courses: They tried to get the oil embargo lifted on terms that would still let them take the territory they wanted, and they prepared for war. The United States demanded that Japan withdraw from China and Indochina, but would very likely have settled for a token withdrawal and a promise not to take more territory. After he became Japan's premier in mid-October, General Tojo Hideki set November 29 as the last day on which Japan would accept a settlement without war. Tojo's deadline, which was kept secret, meant that war was practically certain.

The Japanese army and navy had, in fact, devised a war plan in which they had great confidence. They proposed to make fast sweeps into Burma, Malaya, the East Indies, and the Philippines and, at the same time, set up a defensive perimeter in the central and southwest Pacific. They expected the United States to declare war but not to be willing to fight long or hard enough to win. Their greatest concern was the U.S. Pacific Fleet, based at Pearl Harbor, Hawaii. If it reacted quickly, it could scramble their very tight timetable. As insurance, the Japanese navy undertook to cripple the Pacific Fleet by a surprise air attack.

A few minutes before 8 AM on Sunday, December 7, 1941, Japanese carrier-based aeroplanes struck Pearl Harbor. In a raid lasting less than two hours, they sank or seriously damaged eight battleships and 13 other naval vessels. The U.S. authorities had broken the Japanese diplomatic code and knew an attack was imminent. A warning had been sent from Washington, but, owing to delays in transmission, it arrived after the raid had begun. In one stroke, the Japanese navy scored a brilliant success—and assured the Axis defeat in World War II. The Japanese attack brought the United States into the war on December 8—and brought it in determined to fight to the finish. Germany and Italy declared war on the United States on December 11.

Japanese Conquests In Asia And The Pacific

In the vast area of land and ocean they had marked for conquest, the Japanese seemed to be everywhere at once. Before the end of December, they took British Hong Kong and the Gilbert Islands (now Kiribati) and Guam and Wake Island (U.S. possessions), and they had invaded British Burma, Malaya, Borneo, and the American-held Philippines. British Singapore, long regarded as one of the world's strongest fortresses, fell to them in February

1942, and in March they occupied the Netherlands East Indies and landed on New Guinea. The American and Philippine forces surrendered at Bataan on April 9, and resistance in the Philippines ended with the surrender of Corregidor on May 6.

According to the Japanese plan, it would be time for them to take a defensive stance when they had captured northern New Guinea (an Australian possession), the Bismarck Archipelago, the Gilberts, and Wake Island, which they did by mid-March. But they had done so well that they decided to expand their defensive perimeter north into the Aleutian Islands, east to Midway Island, and south through the Solomon Islands and southern New Guinea. Their first move was by sea, to take Port Moresby on the southeastern tip of New Guinea. The Americans, using their ability to read the Japanese code, had a naval task force on the scene. In the ensuing Battle of the Coral Sea (May 7-8), fought entirely by aircraft carriers, the Japanese were forced to abandon their designs on Port Moresby.

The Russian Front: Summer 1942

In the most immediately critical area of the war, the USSR, the initiative had passed to the Germans again by summer 1942. The Soviet successes in the winter had been followed by disasters in the spring. Setbacks south of Leningrad, near Kharkiv, and in Crimea had cost well more than a half-million men in prisoners alone. The Germans had not sustained such massive losses, but the fighting had been expensive for them too, especially since the Soviets had three times the human resources at their disposal. Moreover, Hitler's overconfidence had led him into a colossal error. He had been so sure of victory in 1941 that he had stopped most kinds of weapons and ammunition production for the army and shifted the industries to work for the air force and navy, with which he proposed to finish off the British. He had resumed production for the army in January 1942, but the flow would not reach the front until late summer. Soviet weapons output, on the other hand, after having dropped low in November and December 1941, had increased steadily since the turn of the year, and the Soviet industrial base also was larger than the German.

Looking ahead to the summer, Hitler knew he could not again mount an all-out, three-pronged offensive. Some of the generals talked about waiting a year until the army could be rebuilt, but Hitler was determined to have the victory in 1942. He had sufficient troops and weapons to bring the southern flank of the eastern front nearly to full strength, and he believed he could compel the Soviet command to sacrifice its main forces trying to defend the coal mines of the Donets Basin and the oil fields of the Caucasus.

The Normandy Invasion

On June 6, 1944, D-Day, the day of invasion for Overlord, the U.S. First Army, under General Omar N. Bradley, and the British Second Army, under General Miles C. Dempsey, established beachheads in Normandy (Normandie), on the French channel coast. The German resistance was strong, and the footholds for Allied armies were not nearly as good as they had expected. Nevertheless, the powerful counterattack with which Hitler had proposed to throw the Allies off the beaches did not materialise, neither on D-Day nor later.

Enormous Allied air superiority over northern France made it difficult for Rommel, who was in command on the scene, to move his limited reserves. Moreover, Hitler became convinced that the Normandy landings were a feint and the main assault would come north of the Seine River. Consequently, he refused to release the divisions he had there and insisted on drawing in reinforcements from more distant areas. By the end of June, Eisenhower had 850,000 men and 150,000 vehicles ashore in Normandy.

The German Surrender

Hitler decided to await the end in Berlin, where he could still manipulate what was left of the command apparatus. Most of his political and military associates chose to leave the capital for places in north and south Germany likely to be out of the Soviet reach. On the afternoon of April 30 Hitler committed suicide in his Berlin bunker. As his last significant official act, he named Grand Admiral Karl Doenitz to succeed him as chief of state.

Doenitz, who had been loyal to Hitler, had no course open to him other than surrender. His representative, General Alfred Jodl, signed an unconditional surrender of all German armed forces at Eisenhower's headquarters in Reims early on May 7. By then the German forces in Italy had already surrendered (on May 2), as had those in Holland, north Germany, and Denmark (May 4). The U.S. and British governments declared May 8 V-E (Victory in Europe) Day. The full unconditional surrender took effect at one minute past midnight after a second signing in Berlin with Soviet participation.

The Defeat Of Japan

Although Japan's position was hopeless by early 1945, an early end to the war was not in sight. The Japanese navy would not be able to come out in force again, but the bulk of the army was intact and was deployed in the home islands and China. The Japanese gave a foretaste of what was yet in store by resorting to kamikaze (Japanese, "divine wind") attacks, or suicide air attacks, during the fighting for Luzon in the Philippines. On January 4-13, 1945, quickly trained kamikaze pilots flying obsolete planes had sunk 17 U.S. ships and damaged 50.

Iwo Jima And Okinawa

While the final assault on Japan awaited reinforcements from Europe, the island-hopping approach march continued, first, with a landing on Iwo Jima (now Iwo To) on February 19. That small, barren island cost the lives of about 6,800 U.S. personnel (including about 6,000 Marines) before it was secured on March 16. Situated almost halfway between the Marianas and Tokyo, the island played an important part: in the air war. Its two airfields provided landing sites for damaged B-29s and enabled fighters to give the bombers cover during their raids on Japanese cities.

On April 1 the U.S. Tenth Army, composed of four army and four marine divisions under General Simon B. Buckner, Jr., landed on Okinawa, 500 km (310 mi) south of the southernmost Japanese island, Kyushu. The Japanese did not defend the beaches. They proposed to make their stand on the southern tip of the island, across which they had constructed three strong lines. The northern three-fifths of the island were secured in less than two weeks, the third line in the south could not be breached until June 14, and the fighting continued to June 21.

Hiroshima And Nagasaki

The next attack was scheduled for Kyushu in November 1945. An easy success seemed unlikely, the Japanese had fought practically to the last man on Iwo Jima, and hundreds of soldiers and civilians had jumped off cliffs at the southern end of Okinawa rather than surrender. Kamikaze planes had sunk 15 naval vessels and damaged 200 off Okinawa.

The Kyushu landing was never made. Throughout the war, the U.S. government and the British, believing Germany was doing the same, had maintained a massive scientific and industrial project to develop an atomic bomb. The chief ingredients, fissionable uranium and Plutonium, had not been available in sufficient quantity before the war in Europe ended. The first bomb was exploded in a test at Almagordo, New Mexico, on July 16, 1945.

Two more bombs had been built, and the possibility arose of using them to convince the Japanese to surrender. President Harry S. Truman decided to allow the bombs to be dropped. For maximum psychological impact, they were used in quick succession, one over Hiroshima on August 6, the other over Nagasaki on August 9. These cities had not previously been bombed, and thus the bombs' damage could be accurately assessed. U.S. estimates put the number killed or missing as a result of the bomb in Hiroshima at 60,000 to 70,000 and in Nagasaki at 40,000. Japanese estimates gave a combined total of

240,000. The USSR declared war on Japan on August 8 and invaded Manchuria the next day.

The Japanese Surrender

On August 14 Japan announced its surrender, which was not quite unconditional because the Allies had agreed to allow the country to keep its emperor. The formal signing took place on September 2 in Tokyo Bay aboard the battleship *Missouri*. The Allied delegation was headed by General MacArthur, who became the military governor of occupied Japan.

Cost Of The War

World War II's basic statistics qualify it as by far the most costly war in history in terms of human casualties and material resources expended. In all, 61 countries with 1.7 billion people, three-fourths of the world's population, took part. A total of 110 million people were mobilized for military service, more than half of those by three countries: the USSR (22 million to- 30 million), Germany (17 million), and the United States (16 million). For the major participants the largest numbers on duty at any one time were as follows: USSR (12,500,000); United States (12,245,000); Germany (10,938,000); British Empire and Commonwealth (8,720,000); Japan (7,193,000); and China (5,000,000).

Most statistics on the war are only estimates. The war's vast and chaotic sweep made uniform record keeping impossible. Some governments lost control of the data, and some resorted to manipulating it for political reasons.

A rough consensus has been reached on the total cost of the war. The human cost is estimated at 55 million dead

—25 million in the military and 30 million civilians. The amount of money spent has been estimated at more than $1 trillion, which makes World War II more expensive than all other wars combined.

Economic Statistics

The United States spent the most money on the war, an estimated $341 billion, including $50 billion for lend-lease supplies, of which $31 billion went to Britain, $11 billion to the Soviet Union, $5 billion to China, and $3 billion to 35 other countries. Germany was next, with $272 billion; followed by the Soviet Union, $192 billion; and then Britain, $120 billion; Italy, $94 billion; and Japan, $56 billion. Except for the United States, however, and some of the less militarily active Allies, the money spent does not come close to being the war's true cost. The Soviet government has calculated that the USSR lost 30 percent of its national wealth, while Nazi exactions and looting were of incalculable amounts in the occupied countries. The full cost to Japan has been estimated at $562 billion. In Germany, bombing and shelling had produced 4 billion cu m (5 billion cu yd) of rubble.

Human Losses

Although the human cost of the war was tremendous, casualty figures cannot always be obtained and often vary widely. Most experts estimate the military and civilian losses of Allied forces at 44 million and those of the Axis at 11 million. The total number of civilian losses includes the 5.6 million to 5.9 million Jews who were killed in the Holocaust. Of all the nations that participated in World War II, the human cost of the war fell heaviest on the USSR, for which the official total, military and civilian, is given as more than 20 million killed. The United States, which had no significant civilian losses, sustained more than 400,000 deaths.

Perhaps the most significant casualty over the long term was the world balance of power. Britain, France, Germany, and Japan ceased to be great powers in the traditional military sense, leaving only two, the United States and the Soviet Union.

Contributed By:**Earl F. Zienke Microsoft ® Encarta ® 2009.** <& 1993-2008 Microsoft Corporation. All rights reserved.

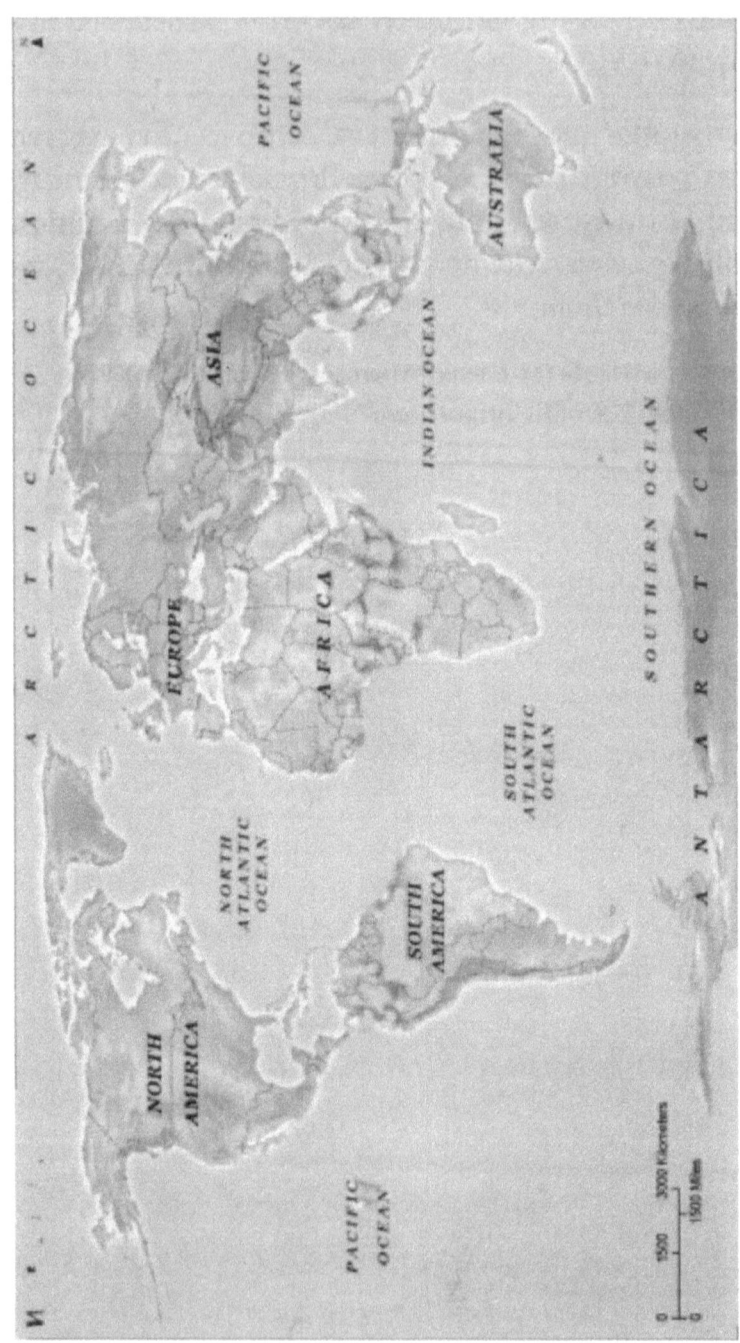

Figure 5.1: Map of the World

Table 5.1: Countries and their sizes

Sizes Of Countries

Rank	Country	Size (sq miles)
1	Russia	6,592,770
2	Canada	3,855,103
3	United States	3,794,083
4	China	3,695,500
5	Brazil	3,300,171
6	Australia	2,966,200
7	India	1,222,243
8	Argentina	1,073,518
9	Kazakhstan	1,049,200
10	Sudan	967,490
11	Algeria	919,595
12	Congo (DRC)	905,365
13	Saudi Arabia	864,900
14	Mexico	758,452
15	Indonesia	735,359
16	Libya	678,400
17	Iran	636,300
18	Mongolia	604,830
19	Peru	496,225
20	Chad	495,755
21	Niger	489,200
22	Angola	481,350
23	Mali	478,841
24	South Africa	470,693
25	Colombia	470,831
26	Ethiopia	437,601
27	Bolivia	424,165
28	Mauritania	398,100
29	Egypt	385,229
30	Tanzania	364,900
31	Nigeria	356,669
32	Venezuela	353,841
33	Namibia	318,252
34	Mozambique	308,642
35	Pakistan	307,374
36	Turkey	300,948
37	Chile	292,135
38	Zambia	290,586
39	Myanmar	261,218

40	Afghanistan	251,825
41	Somalia	246,200
42	Central Africa Republic	240,324
43	Ukraine	233,100
44	Madagascar	226,658
45	Kenya	224,961
46	Botswana	224,607
47	France	210,026
48	Yemen	203,850
49	Thailand	198,115
50	Spain	195,364
51	Turkmenistan	188,500
52	Cameroon	183,569
53	Papua New Guinea	178,704
54	Morocco	175,186
55	Sweden	173,732
56	Uzbekistan	172,700
57	Iraq	169,235
58	Paraguay	157,048
59	Zimbabwe	150,873
60	Norway	148,896
61	Japan	145,884
62	Germany	137,827
63	Congo (ROC)	132,000
64	Finland	130,559
65	Vietnam	128,066
66	Malaysia	127,320
67	Cote D Ivoire	121,503
68	Poland	120,728
69	Oman	119,500
70	Italy	116,341
71	Philippines	116,000
72	Burkina Faso	105,900
73	Ecuador	105,037
74	New Zealand	104,454
75	Gabon	103,347
76	Guinea	94,926
77	United Kindgom	94,251
78	Uganda	93,965
79	Ghana	92,090
80	Romania	92,013
81	Laos	91,430
82	Guyana	83,000
83	Belarus	80,153

84	Kyrgyzstan	76,640
85	Senegal	75,955
86	Syria	71,498
87	Cambodia	69,898
88	Uruguay	68,037
89	Tunisia	63,482
90	Suriname	63,037
91	Bangladesh	56,977
92	Nepal	56,827
93	Tajikistan	55,250
94	Grecce	50,949
95	Nicaragua	49,998
96	Eritrea	46,774
97	North Korea	46,540
98	Malawi	45,747
99	Cuba	44,218
100	Benin	43,484
101	Honduras	43,433
102	Bulgaria	42,855
103	Guatamela	42,542
104	Iceland	39,800
105	South Korea	38,328
106	Liberia	38,250
107	Hungary	35,919
108	Portugal	35,855
109	Jordan	34,378
110	Serbia	34,146
111	Azerbaijan	33,400
112	Austria	32,378
113	United Arab Emirates	32,600
114	Czech Republic	30,450
115	Panama	29,157
116	Sierra Leone	27,699
117	Ireland	27,133
118	Georgia	26,900
119	Sri Lanka	25,332
120	Lithuania	25,200
121	Latvia	24,600
122	Togo	21,925
123	Croatia	21,819
124	Bosnia and Herzegovina	19,741
125	Costa Rica	19,714
126	Slovakia	18,933
127	Dominican Republic	18,700

128	Bhutan	18,100
129	Estonia	17,462
130	Denmark	16,639
131	Netherlands, The	16,033
132	Switzerland	15,940
133	Guinea-Bissau	13,948
134	Moldovia	13,000
135	Belgium	11,787
136	Lesotho	11,720
137	Armenia	11,500
138	Albania	11,100
139	Equatorial Guinea	10,831
140	Burundi	10,747
141	Haiti	10,714
142	Solomon Islands	10,639
143	Rwanda	10,169
144	F.Y.R.O. Macedonia	9,928
145	Djibouti	8,958
146	Belize	8,867
147	Israel	8,473
148	El Salvador	8,124
149	Slovenia	7,820
150	Fiji Islands	7,095
151	Kuwait	6,880
152	Swaziland	6,704
153	Timor-Leste	5,743
154	Bahamas The	5,382
155	Montenegro	5,333
156	Vanuatu	4,707
157	Quatar	4,412
158	Gambia The	4,361
159	Jamaica	4,244
160	Leanon	4,036
161	Cyprus	3,572
162	Brunei	2,226
163	Trinidad and Tobago	1,980
164	Cape Verde	1,557
165	Samoa	1,093
166	Luxemburg	999
167	Mauritius	788
168	Comoros	719
169	Sao Tome and Principe	387
170	Kiribati	313
171	Dominican	290

172	Tonga	290
173	Baharain	273
174	Macronesia, Fed. State of	271
175	Singapore	264
176	St. Lucia	238
177	Palau	188
178	Andorra	181
179	Seychelles	175
180	Antigua and Berbuda	171
181	Barbados	166
182	St. Vincent and Bernadines	150
183	Grenada	133
184	Malta	122
185	Maldives	115
186	St. Kits and Nevies	104
187	Marshall Islands	70
188	Liechtenstein	62
189	San Marino	24
190	Tuvalu	10
191	Nauru	8
192	Monaco	0.77
193	Vatican City	0.17

Table 5.2: Countries and their Population

World Population

Country	Population	Country	Population
Africa	**991189**	Sierra Leone	5 132
Algeria	34 179	Somalia	9 832
Angola	12 799	South Africa	49 052
Benin	8792	Sudan	41 088
Botswana	1 991	Swaziland	1 337
Burkina Faso	15746	Tanzania	41 049
Burundi	9 511	Togo	6 032
Cameroon	18879	Tunisia	10486
Cape Verde	429	Uganda	32 370-
Central African Rep.	4 511	Zambia	11 863
Chad	10 329	Zimbabwe	11393
Comoros	752		
Congo, Dem Rep of	4013	**North America**	**534 187**
Congo, Rep of	68 693	Anguilla	14 •*
Cote d'Ivoire	20 617	Antigua and Barbuda	86
Djibouti	725	Aruba	103
Egypt	78 867	Bahamas	308
Equatorial Guinea	633	Barbados	285—
Eritrea	5 647	Belize	308—
Ethiopia	85 237	Bermuda	68
Gabon	1 515	Canada	33 487
Gambia, The	1 778	Cayman Islands	49
Ghana	23 888	Costa Rica	4 254
Guinea	10058	Cuba	11 424
Guinea-Bissau	1 534	Dominica	73
Kenya	39 003	Dominican Republic	9 650
Lesotho	.2 131	El Salvador	7185
Liberia	3 442	Grenada	90
Libya	6 324	Guadeloupe	453[1]
Madagascar	20 654	Guatemala	13277
Malawi	15 029	Haiti	9 036
Mali	13 443	Honduras	7 834
Mauritania	3 129	Jamaica	2 826
Mauritius	1 284	Martinique	398[1]
Mayotte	224	Mexico	111 212
Morocco	32 285	Montserrat	5
Mozambique	21 669	Neth Antilles	227
Namibia	.2 109	Nicaragua	5 891
Niger	15 306	Panama	3 360
•Nigeria	149229	Puerto Rico	3 966
Rwanda	10746	Saint Kitts and Nevis	40
Sahara, Western	405	Saint Lucia	160
Saint Helena	8	Saint Pierre and Miq'n	7
Sao Tome and Principe	213	Saint Vincent	105
Senegal	13 712	Trinidad and Tobago	1 230
Seychelles	87	Turks and Caicos Islands	23

United States.......	307 212	Myanmar..........	48 138
Virgin Islands, UK........	24	Nepal...............	28 563
Virgin Islands, U.S.	110	Oman	3418
South America	**392 560**	Philippines...........	97 977
Argentina	40 914	Qatar....................	833
Bolivia...............	9 775	Saudi Arabia	28 687
Brazil...............	198 739	Singapore...........	4658
Chile...............	16 602	Sri Lanka	21 325
Colombia	43 677	Syria	21 763
Ecuador...........	14 573	Taiwan...............	22 974
Falkland Islands	3	Tajikistan.............	7 849
French Guiana..........	191	Thailand.............	65 998
Guyana	753	Timor, East...........	1 132
Paraguay.............	6 996	Turkey...............	76 806
Peru...............	29 547	Turkmenistan.........	5 180
Suriname...............	481	United Arab Emirates..	4 885
Uruguay.............	3 494	Uzbekistan..........	27 607
Venezuela...........	26 815	Vietnam	88 577
		West Bank and Gaza...	4 013
Asia	**4 065 409**	Yemen...............	22 858
Afghanistan	28 395		
Armenia	2 967	**Europe**	**732 000**
Azerbaijan............	8 239	Albania	3 639
Bahrain...............	729	Andorra	84
Bangladesh........	156 051	Austria	8210
Bhutan...............	691	Belarus............	9 685
Brunei...............	388	Belgium	10414
Cambodia...........	14 494	Bosnia and Hercegovina..	4 613
China (Mainland)..	1 338 613	Bulgaria	7 205
China (Hong Kong)....	7 055	Channel Islands	157
China (Macau)...........	560	Croatia	4 489
Georgia...............	4 616	Cyprus...............	1 085
India............	1 156 898	Czech Republic	10212
Indonesia..........	240 272	Denmark............	5 501
Iran	66 429	Estonia	1 299
Iraq	28 946	Faroes...................	49
Israel...............	7 234	Finland	5 250
Japan	127 079	France............	64 420
Jordan...............	6 269	Germany.	82 330
Kazakhstan...........	15 399	Gibraltar.	29
Korea, North	22 665	Greece.	10737
Korea, South	48 509	Greenland	58
Kuwait...............	2 693	Hungary	9 906
Kyrgyzstan	5 432	Iceland	307
Laos..................	6 834	Ireland...............	4 203
Lebanon	4017	Isle of Man.	77
Malaysia............	25 716	Italy.................	58 126
Maldives	396	Latvia.	2 232
Mongolia	3 041	Liechtenstein	35

Lithuania.	3 555	**Oceania. ....**	**34 676**
Luxembourg	492	Australia	21 263
Macedonia, FYR of	2 067	Cook Islands	12
Malta	405	Fiji	945
Moldova	4 321	Fr Polynesia............	287
Monaco	33	Guam	178
Montenegro	672	Kiribati................	113
Netherlands.........	16 716	Marshall Islands.........	65
Norway	4 661	Micronesia, Fed St of. ...	107
Poland.............	38 413	Nauru	14
Portugal	10 708	New Caledonia	227
Romania.......	22215	New Zealand.........	4 213
Russia	140 041	Niue	1
San Marino	30	Norfolk Island	2
Serbia	7 379	Northern Mariana Is.	51
Slovakia	5 463	Papua New Guinea	5 941
Slovenia	2 006	Pitcairn .... [2]	
Spain.	46158	Samoa	220
Sweden.	9 060	Samoa, American.	66
Switzerland	7 604	Solomon Islands.	596
Ukraine............	45 700	Tonga.................	121
United Kingdom	61 113	Tuvalu................	12
Vatican	1	Vanuatu	219
		Wallis and Futuna Is.	15

Source: The Economist (Of London) Desk Diary 2011

Table 5.3: Desert and their Sizes

Largest Deserts in the World

Desert	Location	Area[1] sqKm
Sahara	Northern Africa	9,100,000
Gobi	Mongolia/Northeastern China	1,300,000
Patagonian	Argentina	670,000
Rub' al Khali	Southern Arabian peninsula	650,000
Great Sandy	Northwestern Australia	390,500
Great Victoria	Southwestern Australia	390,500
Chihuahuan	Mexico/Southwestern United States	360,000
Taklamakan	China	360,000
Sonoran	United States	310,000
Kalahari	Namibia	260,000
Kyzyl Kum	Uzbekistan	260,000
Thar	India/Pakistan	260,000
Simpson	Australia	200,000
Mojave	United States	140,00

[1] Desert areas are very approximate, because clear physical boundaries may not occour

Microsoft ® Encarta ® 2009. © 1993-2008 Microsoft Corporation. All rights reserved.

Table 5.4: Rivers and their Lengths

River Lengths

North And Central America	Kilometres	Miles
Mississippi Missouri	6,019	3,740
Mackenzie	4,250	2,640
Missouri	3,969	2,466
Mississippi	3,779	2,348
Yukon	3,485	1,980
St Lawrence	3,058	1,900
Rio Grande	2,870	1,785
Nelson-Saskatchewan	2,570	1,600
Arkansas	2,348	1,459
Colorado	2,333	1,450
Columbia	2,250	1,400
Maladera	3,200	1,990
Sao Francisco	2,900	1800
Para-Tocantins	2,750	1700
Paraguay	2,600	1615
Orinoco	2,500	1,555
Maranon	1,609	1000
Magdalena	1,550	963

Africa	Kilometres	Miles
Nile	6,695	4,160
Congo (Zaire)	4667	2,900
Niger	4030	2,505
Zambezi	2650	1650
Shabeelle (Shebele)	2490	1550
Orange	1860	1155
Asia	Kilometres	Miles
Chang Jiang	6,380	3,965
Ob'Irtsh	5,570	3,460
Yenisey Angara	5,550	3,450
Huang He	5,464	3,395
Mekong	4,425	2,750
Amur	4,416	2,744
Lena	4400	2,730
Indus	3,180	1,975
Syrdar'ya	3,078	1,913

Europe	Kilometres	Miles
Volga	3,688	2290
Danube	2,850	1770
Dnepr	2,285	1420
Don	1,870	1162
Pechora	1,809	1424
Rhine	1,320	820
Elbe	1,159	720
Vistula	1014	630
Loire	1012	629
Tagus	1006	625
Meuse (M...	925	575
Oder	909	565
Seine	761	473
severn	354	220

Australasia	Kilometres	Miles
Murray-Darling	3750	2330

Table 5.5: World Production of Food and Cash Crops

Food and tobacco crops ('000 tonnes 2006)

Crop / Country	Production	Crop / Country	Production
Wheat		**Barley**	
World	605,946	World	138643
China	104,470	Russia	18154
India	69,350	Germany	11967
United States	57,298	Ukraine	11316
Russia	45,006	Canada	10004
Oats		**Rye**	
World	23 101	World	13,261
Russia	4,880	Russia	2,965
Canada	3,602	Germany	2644
United States	1,361	Poland	2621
China	1,160	Belarus	1022
Maize		**Rice**	
World	695228	World	634606
United States	267598	China	184070
China	145625	India	136510
Brazil	42632	Indonesia	54400
Mexico	21765	Bangladesh	43729
Sorghum		**Millet**	
World	56485	World	31781
Nigeria	9866	India	10100
United State	7050	Nigeria	7705
India	7240	Niger	3200
Mexico	5486	China	1321
Cassava		**Potatoes**	
World	226337	World	315100
Nigeria	45721	China	70,338
Brazil	26713	Rusia	385,73
Thailand	22,584	India	23910
Indonesia	19927	Ukraine	19,467
Sweet potatoes		**Sugar**	
World	123510	World	139237
China	100222	Brazil	29500
Nigeria	3462	India	21073
Uganda	2628	China	12319
Indonesia	1851	United States	8456

Tomatoes		Oranges	
World	125,543	World	61795
China	32540	Brazil	18059
United States	11250	United States	9000
Turkey	9885	Mexico	3980
India	3637	India	3469
Bananas		**Apples**	
World	70756	World	63805
India	11710	China	26065
Brazil	7088	United States	4568
China	7053	Iran	2661
Philippines	6795	Poland	2305
Grapes		**Coffee**	
World	69953	World	7843
Italy	8325	Brazil	2592
France	6693	Vietnam	853
Spain	6401	Colombia	696
China	6375	Indonesia	653
Cocoa		**Tea**	
World	4059	World	3649
Cote d'Ivoire	1400	China	1049
Ghana	734	India	893
Indonesia	580	Sri Lanka	311
Nigeria	485	Kenya	311
Tobacco		**Fibers ('000 tonnes; 2006**	
World	7843	**Cotton**	
Brazil	2592	World	24836
Vietnam	853	China	6730
Colombia	696	United States	4498
Indonesia	653	India	3563
		Pakistan	2186
Wool		**Jute**	
World	2194	World	3111
Australia	519	India	2041
China	389	Bangladesh	801
New Zealand	210	China	87
Iran	75	Thailand	31
Sisal		**silk**	
World	428	World	427
Brazil	248	China	300
Tanzania	27	India	77
Mexico	27	Uzbekistan	20
Kenya	25	Iran	6

Table 5.6: World Natural Resources Production

World Natural Resources

Metals		Pig iron	
Iron ore (million tones; 2007)		(million tones; 2007)	
World	1900	World	940
China	600	China	465
Brazil..................	360	Japan	87
Australia	320	Russia	50
India	160	United States ...	36
Bauxite (million tones; 2007)		**Copper** ('000 tones; 2007)	
World	190	World	15 600
Austria	64	Chile	5 700
China	62	Peru	1 200
Guinea	24	United States	1 190
Brazil	14	China	920
Aluminium ('000 tones; 2007)		**Lead** ('000 tones; 2007)	
World	38000	World	3550
China	12,000	China	1320
Russia	4200	Australia	640
Canada	3100	United States	430
United States	2600	Peru	330
Zinc ('000 tones; 2007)		**Tin** ('000 tones; 2007)	
World	10 500	World	300
China	2 800	China	130
Peru	1 500	Indonesia..................	85
Australia	1 400	Peru	38
United States	749	Bolivia.....................	18
Nickel ('000 tones; 2007)		**Antimony** ('000 tones; 2007)	
World	1 660	World	135
Russia	322	China	110
Canada	258	Bolivia	7
Australia	180	South Africa	6
Austria............	145	Russia	4
Molybdenum ('000 tones; 2007)		**Platinum** (tones; 2007)	
World	187	World	3080
United States...........	59	South Africa	1212
China	46	Russia	595
Chile	41	Canada	210
Peru....................	18	Zimbabwe............	203

Crude Oil (Mn tones, 2006)		Natural gas (Mn tones oil equiv. 06)	
World	4075	World	2487
Saudi Arabia	550	Russia	538
Russia	480	United States	473
United States	312	Canada	167
Iran	243	United Kingdom	79
Rubber natural ('000 tones; 2006)		**Rubber synthetic** ('000 tones; 2006)	12571
World	9255	World	2462
Thailand	2968	United States	1827
Indonesia	2454	China	1612
Malaysia	1211	Japan	1180
India	857	Russia	
Olives ('000 tones; 2006)		**Groundnuts** ('000 tones; 2005/06)	
World	15100	World	33870
Spain	5355	China	14340
Italy	3551	India	7200
Greece	2300	United States	2210
Lukky	1650	Nigeria	1520
Antimony ('000 tones; 2006/07)		**Soya beans** ('000 tones; 2006/07)	
World	46,800	World	235 540
China	12650	United States	86 770
Canada	9000	Brazil	59 000
India	5800	Argentina	42 200
Germany	5340	China	15 970

CHAPTER SIX

Know The Universe

In a nutshell, the Universe is "the whole of space and everything in it, including the earth, the planets and the stars; a system of stars, planets, etc, in space outside our own" (Oxford Advanced Learners Dictionary, 7th Edition, Oxford University Press 2006)

2. The Universe is infinite in space and that about 14 billion years ago, the Universe began as an explosive event, resulting in a hot, dense expanding sea of matter and energy. This event is known as the big bang. About 4.6 billion years ago, our solar system formed. A Solar system consists of a central star orbited by planets or smaller rocky bodies. In our Solar System, the central star is the Sun. It holds all the planets, including Earth in their orbits and provides light and energy necessary for life. Our Solar System is just one of many. It contains the sun, planets (of which Earth is third from the Sun), and the planets satellites. It also contains asteroids, comets, and interplanetary dust and gas.

Planets And Their Satellites

Until the end of the 18th century, humans knew of five planets — Mercury, Venus, Mars, Jupiter, and Saturn — in addition to Earth. When viewed without a telescope, planets appear to be dots of light in the sky. They shine steadily, while stars seem to twinkle. Twinkling results from turbulence in Earth's atmosphere. Stars are so far away that they appear as tiny points of light. A moment of turbulence can change that light for a fraction of a second. Even though they look the same size as stars to unaided human eyes, planets are close enough that they take up more space in the sky than stars do. The disks of planets are big enough to average out variations in light caused by turbulence and therefore do not twinkle.

Between 1781 and 1930, astronomers found three more planets—Uranus, Neptune, and Pluto. This brought the total number of planets in our solar system to nine. However, in 2006 the International Astronomical Union (IAU)—the official body that names objects in the solar system—reclassified Pluto as a dwarf planet. The IAU rulings reduced the number of official planets in the solar system to eight. In order of increasing distance from the Sun, the planets in our solar system are Mercury, Venus, Earth, Mars, Jupiter, Saturn, Uranus, and Neptune.

Astronomers call the inner planets—Mercury, Venus, Earth, and Mars—the terrestrial planets. Terrestrial (from the Latin word *terra*, meaning "Earth") planets are Earthlike in that they have solid, rocky surfaces. The next group of planets—Jupiter, Saturn, Uranus, and Neptune—is called the Jovian planets, or the giant planets. The word Jovian has the same Latin root as the word Jupiter. Astronomers call these planets the Jovian planets because they resemble Jupiter in that they are giant, massive planets made almost entirely of gas. The mass of Jupiter, for example, is 318 times the mass of Earth. The Jovian planets have no solid surfaces, although they probably have rocky cores several times more massive than Earth. Rings of chunks of ice and rock surround each of the

Jovian planets. The rings around Saturn are the most familiar.

Pluto is tiny, with a mass about one five-hundredth the mass of Earth. Pluto seems out of place, with its tiny, solid body out beyond the giant planets. Many astronomers believe that Pluto is just one of a group of icy objects in the outer solar system. These objects orbit in a part of the solar system called the Kuiper Belt. In 2006 the International Astronomical Union (IAU) reclassified Pluto as a dwarf planet because it had a rounded shape from effects of its own gravity but it was not massive enough to have cleared the region of its orbit of other bodies. Other dwarf planets in the solar system include Eris, an icy body slightly larger than Pluto that also orbits in part of the Kuiper Belt, and Ceres, a rocky body that orbits in the asteroid belt.

Most of the planets have moons, or satellites. Earth's Moon has a diameter about one-fourth the diameter of Earth. Mars has two tiny chunks of rock, Phobos and Deimos, each only about 10 km (about 6 mi) across. Jupiter has more than 60 satellites. The largest four, known as the Galilean satellites, are Io, Europa, Ganymede, and Callisto. Ganymede is even larger than the planet Mercury. Saturn has more than 50 satellites. Saturn's largest moon, Titan, is also larger than the planet Mercury and is enshrouded by a thick, opaque, smoggy atmosphere. Uranus has nearly 30 known moons, and Neptune has at least 13 moons. Some of the dwarf planets also have satellites. Pluto has three moons; the largest is called Charon. Charon is more than half as big as Pluto. Eris has a small moon named Dysnomia.

Comets And Asteroids

Comets and asteroids are rocky and icy bodies that are smaller than planets. The distinction between comets, asteroids, and other small bodies in the solar system is a little fuzzy, but generally a comet is icier than an asteroid and has a more elongated orbit. The orbit of a comet takes it close to the Sun, then back into the outer solar system. When comets near the Sun, some of their ice turns from solid material into gas, releasing some of their dust. Comets have long tails of glowing gas and dust when they are near the Sun. Asteroids are rockier bodies and usually have orbits that keep them at always about the same distance from the Sun.

The Sun

The Sun is the nearest star to Earth and is the centre of the solar system. It is only 8 light-minutes away from Earth, meaning light takes only eight minutes to travel from the Sun to Earth. The next nearest star is 4 light-years away, so light from this star, Proxima Centauri (part of the triple star Alpha Centauri), takes four years to reach Earth. The Sun's closeness means that the light and other energy we get from the Sun dominate Earth's environment and life. The Sun also provides a way for astronomers to study stars. They can see details and layers of the Sun that are impossible to see on more distant stars.

Source; Microsoft Corporation.

Table 6.2 provides detailed data on all the nine planets of our Solar system whilst Table 6.3 provides Lunar data.

Source: The Times Comprehensive Atlas of the World-10th Edition

The Sun is an apparently quite ordinary yellow dwarf main sequence star, yet it is almost entirely to the Sun that we owe our light and warmth. The Sun condensed some 4600 million years ago; it is about 150 million km away from the Earth, and has a diameter of 140,000 km compared with the Earth's 12,756 km. The Sun is mostly hydrogen with about 15% helium and only trace proportions of other elements.

Earth

Earth is the largest and densest of the Inner Planets. Created some 4,500 million years ago, the core, rocky mantle and crust are similar in structure to Venus. The Earth's core is composed almost entirely of iron and oxygen compounds which exist in a molten state at temperatures of around 5,000°C. Earth is the only planet with vast quantities of life-sustaining water, with the oceans covering 70.8% of its surface (due to climate change, this figure is bound to increase). The actions of plate tectonics has created vast mountain ranges and is responsible for volcanic activity. The moon is Earth's only natural satellite with a diameter of over one-quarter of that of the earth, makes the Earth-Moon system a near double planet.

Source: The Times Comprehensive Atlas of the World-10th Edition

Earth has over 6 billion inhabitants, though it is believed that there may be other forms of life in the universe.

Earthlike Planets

The Earthlike planets are those dance planets with metallic cores and silicate mantles and crusts which condensed closest to the sun. As well as Mercury, Venus, Earth and Mars most scientists would include Earth's Moon in this category.

Mercury

Mercury is the nearest planet to the Sun, and its rotation is so strongly under the influence of the sun's gravity that it spins exactly 3 times for every 2 orbits around the sun.

Venus

Venus is the most similar planet to Earth in both volume and mass. However, it has a dense atmosphere of 96% carbon dioxide mixed with nitrogen, oxygen, sulphur dioxide and water vapour which hides the surface under permanent cloud and maintains, through the greenhouse effect, a mean surface temperature of about 480°C.

Mars

Mars, for long the favourite candidate for extraterrestrial life within the solar system has now been revealed to have a hostile surface environment. There is a thin atmosphere of about 95% carbon dioxide mixed with nitrogen, argon, oxygen, water vapour and other minor constituents. There are polar caps of semipermanent water ice and ephemeral solid carbon dioxide which sublimate during summer so that the atmospheric pressure varies from about 7 to 10 millibars. Day and night surface temperatures vary between about -120°C and - 20°C.   Mars has two small satellites, each less than about 25km across, which are probably captured asteroids.

Gas Giants

The Gas Giants orbit much further from the sun than the Earth-like planets and are much richer in volatiles, having outer layers rich in hydrogen and smaller quantities of helium, methane and ammonia.

Jupiter

Jupiter is the largest planet and is more than twice as massive as all the other planets put together. It has at least 16 satellites and a debris ring system (much less spectacular than that of its famous neighbour, Saturn) at about 50,000 km above the cloud tops.

Saturn

Saturn is the least dense of the planets and is similar to Jupiter in many ways. It has a comparable, though less dramatically stormy, atmosphere situated above a layer of liquid molecular hydrogen and helium about 30,000 km thick, which is distorted due to the planet's rotation to give Saturn almost twice the degree of polar flattening seen on Jupiter.

Saturn has the most splendid ring structure in the solar system. The rings are thought to be made of mostly icy debris, from about 10m down to a few microns in size, derived from the break-up of a satellite which strived too close of Saturn.

Uranus

Comparatively little was known about Uranus until the space probe Voyager 2 flew by it in January 1986. It has a cloud cover more featureless than either Jupiter or Saturn. It consists mostly of hydrogen.

Neptune

Neptune provided a number of surprises when Voyager 2 flew by on 24 August 1989, passing within 500km of the planet's north pole. The atmosphere is mainly hydrogen and helium with some methane. The planet rotates in just over 16 hours, the large spot in 18.3 hours and the small spot in 16.0 hours. The magnetic axis is inclined at 22° to the axis of rotation.

Pluto

Pluto's eccentric orbit has brought it nearer than Neptune from 1983 until the year 2000.

Earth's Moon

The Moon, with a diameter of 3,476km, is the smallest of the Earth-like planets. Being the closest extraterrestrial body it was the first to be mapped.

Space Flight

For a spacecraft to escape from the gravitational pull of the Earth it must be travelling in excess of 40,000 Km per hour. A less powerful launch will be it in orbit. In a very low circular orbit 200 Km high a satellite will orbit the Earth in a period of 90 minutes at 29,0000 Km per hour. At greater altitudes the orbital speed decreases and the period increases so that at a height of about 35,700 Km a satellite takes exactly 24 hours to complete an orbit at 11,300 Km per hour. If this satellite is situated over the Equator, its position in the sky will change very little and it is said to be in geostationary orbit. Although small solid-propellent rockets had existed for hundreds of years, the space age can be said to have begun with the German A4/V2 rocket. By 1944, following a ballistic trajectory that took it to the fringes of space, it was carrying a payload of a tonne over distances up to 250 Km. Military considerations have continued to set the pace for more powerful rockets and specialist Earth satellites but space exploration has benefited greatly as a result.

On 4 October 1957 the USSR (Union of Soviet Socialist Republics) launched the first artificial satellite, sputnik I. The first American satellite, Explorer I, followed within four months. The Russian lead in what developed into a space race was maintained by the first pictures of the far side of the moon (Luna 3, 1959) and the first manned space flight (Yuri Gagarin, 1961), whereas the Americans at the same time were developing specialist satellites such as TIROS I (the first weather satellite) and ECHO I the first communications satellite), all launched in 1960. On 20 July, 1969 the first manned landing was made using the Saturn V rocket (US astronauts Armstrong, Aldrin and Collins, Apollo xi).

The Russian manned programme continued with longer flights in Earth orbit and the launch of their first space Salyut-Space stations (from 1971) while their lunar programme continued with robot exploration and the return of small samples to Earth.

Source - The Times Atlas of the World (Comprehensive Edition), 1998.

Table 6.1: Lunar Data

Earth/Moon Mass Ratio	Me/mm81 3015
Density (mean)	3.34g/cm³
Synodic Month(new Moon to new Moon)	29.530588d
Sideral Month (fixed star to fixed star)	27 321661 days
Inclination of Lunar orbit to ecliptic	5°8'43"
Inclination of equator to ecliptic	1°40'32"
Inclination of Lunar orbit To Earth's equator	18 3°to28.6°
Distance fromMoon to Earth (mean)	(238 860mi)
Optical libration in longitude	±7.6°
Optical libration in latitude	±6.7°
Magnitude (mean of full Moon)	-12.7
Temperature	-153°C to +134°C
	(-244°F to +273°F)
Escape velocity	2.38km/sec (1.48mi/sec)
Diameter of Moon	3 476km (2 160mi)
Surface gravity	162.2cm/sec²
Orbital velocity	1.024km/sec (Moon) 0.64mi/sec
	29.6km/sec (Earth) 18.5 mi/sec

Table 6.2: Physical and Astronomical data of Earth's Solar System

	Sun	Mercury	Venus	Earth	(Moon)	Mars	Jupiter	Saturn	Uranus	Neptune	Pluto
Mass (Earth =1)	333400	0.055	0.815	1(5.97 10^{24}kg)	0.012	0.107	317.8	95.2	14.5	17.2	0.003
Volume (Earth = 1)	1306000	0.06	0.88	1	0.020	0.150	1323	752	64	54	0.007
Density (Water = 1)	1.41	3.43	5.24	5.52	3.34	3.94	1.33	0.70	1.30	1.64	2.0
Equatorial diameter (km)	1392000	4878	12.104	12756	3.476	6794	42800	120000	52000	48400	2302
Polar flattering	0	0	0	0.003	0	0.005	0.065	0.108	0.060	0.021	0
"Surface" gravity (Earth =1)	279	0.37	0.88	1	0.16	0.38	2.69	1.19	0.93	1.22	0.05
Number of satellites Greater than 100km diameter	-	0	0	1	-	0	7	13	7	6	1
Total number of satellites	-	0	0	1	-	2	16	17	15	8	1
Period of rotation (in Earth days)	25.38	58.65	-243 (retrograde)	23hr 56mm 4 secs	27.32	1.03	0.414	0.426	-0.74 (retrograde)	0.67	-6.93 (retrograde)
Length of year (in Earth days and years)	-	88 days	224.7 days	365 26 days	-	687 days	1186 years	2946 years	8401 years	164.8 years	247.7 years
Distance from Sun (max) Mkm	-	69.7	109	152.1	-	249.1	815.7	1507	3004	4537	7.375

	Sun	Mercury	Venus	Earth	(Moon)	Mars	Jupiter	Saturn	Uranus	Neptune	Pluto
Distance from Sun (mean) Mkm	-	45.9	107.4	147.1	-	206.7	740.9	1347	2735	4456	4.425
Distance from Sun (mean) Mkm	-	57.9	108.9	149.6	-	227.9	778.3	1427	2670	4497	5900
Mean orbital velocity km/sec	-	47.9	35.0	29.8	-	24.1	13.1	9.6	6.8	5.4	4.7
Inclination of equator to orbit plane	7.25	0.0	177.3	23.45	6.68	25.19	3.12	26.73	97.86	29.56	122°
Inclination or orbit to ecliptic	-	7.01	3.39	0	5.15	1.85	1.30	2.48	0.77	1.77	17.13°

www.ingramcontent.com/pod-product-compliance
Lightning Source LLC
Chambersburg PA
CBHW050902300426
44111CB00010B/1349